2—

LITTLE BOOK OF

Melvyn Harris

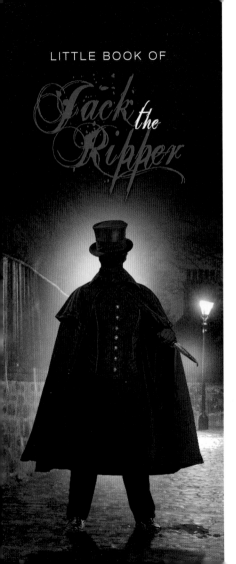

LITTLE BOOK OF

Jack the Ripper

First published in the UK in 2014

© Demand Media Limited 2014

www.demand-media.co.uk

Printed and bound in Europe

ISBN 978-1-910270-01-1

Contents

Introduction

JACK THE RIPPER: why does that name still fascinate? He was not the first serial sexual murderer, as many imagine, and his crimes were quite overshadowed by earlier killers. The Texas Ripper alone killed nine women between Christmas 1884 and Christmas 1885, and all his killings were many times more brutal. So what was it about Jack's murders that made them so special? The short answer is: the time, the place and the publicity.

He struck at a time when London's police were the subject of intense debate; he struck in the capital city that claimed to be the very centre of the civilized world; and his butchery attracted press coverage that was unprecedented.

Those earlier murders in Austin, Texas, were hardly known, even in America; but the London murders became notorious throughout the world. And in the telling, the crimes became more horrifying. They were imagined to have spanned many years; the number of victims was increased from the actual five Ripper murders to fifteen or more.

The terror evoked by the Ripper was so great that lone women throughout Britain double-barred their doors long after he had retired. For years after, he was pictured as roaming throughout the Midlands, the North and beyond. There was a reported sighting in Belfast, another in Cork; and even one old lady in the far-off Orkneys testified that she lay petrified each night, dreading a visit from the fiend.

The time came, eventually, when

> "What manner of man could have mutilated with such taunting, callous indifference? How did he evade capture? Was there a cover-up?"

everyone accepted that the killings had finished, but even that failed to put the case to rest. Far from it; since no one had faced trial, a perplexing mystery was spawned. What manner of man could have mutilated with such taunting, callous indifference? How did he evade capture? Was there a cover-up?

The police were never able to answer these questions. They were crippled by unsophisticated notions of criminal mentality. In their minds there was no room for a cold, calculating killer who planned his stalks. He had to be a homicidal maniac, subject to outbursts of uncontrollable passion.

The Whitechapel murders came at a time when popular discontent with the Metropolitan Police was at a peak. A recently appointed Chief Commissioner, Sir Charles Warren, headed the force. Sir Charles was an army man, first and foremost. He filled five new senior police posts with army officers and introduced military discipline into a civilian force.

Warren quickly made enemies. He clashed with the Home Secretary Charles Matthews over the everyday running of the force, and he antagonized the trades unionists, radicals and labour bodies of the day, by closing Trafalgar Square to all meetings and demonstrations.

On 13 November 1887 this resulted in a head-on clash between demonstrators and 4,300 police aided by armed cavalry and foot-soldiers. One demonstrator died; 300 others were injured and Warren became a hated figure to thousands of ordinary people. He was never allowed to forget 'Bloody Sunday, so he entered 1888 handicapped by press hostility and public anger.

When the Ripper murders erupted and the killer remained free, hostile newspapers sniped away at Warren unmercifully. They branded him as inept, inflexible, and damaging to police morale. Even the man he chose to head the CID, Robert Anderson, was damned by association, and ridiculed for going on a 'rest cure' in Switzerland on the very eve of the first murder. Incredibly

INTRODUCTION

enough he remained abroad until well after the fourth murder, leaving Chief Inspector Donald Swanson to stand in for him. But the public heard and saw little of Swanson. The most visible of all the Ripper-hunters was the well-liked Inspector Frederick George Abberline. Abberline knew the East End and its denizens intimately, for fourteen years he had even served in Whitechapel itself.

In the 1900s all three policemen would air their views on the identity of the Ripper, each would clash with the others; but in 1888 not one of them had the slightest idea that the man they were looking for had moved around in police circles for almost twenty years.

For the first time, in this book, this man is investigated in full. He is unique. He is not a madman, or a fantasy candidate but an authentic suspect of the time. His indictment is based on solid evidence, without recourse to faked documents or journalists' inventions. Consider his background, his cold-blooded personality, his strange actions, sayings and writings. Look without prejudice or preconceptions at the facts and you will see the true face of - Jack the Ripper, Master of the Killing Fields.

Chapter 1

The Killing Fields

Ghastly Murder! Revolting and Mysterious Murder! East End Horrors! Dreadful Mutilation of a Woman! These were some of the garish newspaper headlines that petrified all England in 1888. Headlines that shrieked out the harrowing tidings of a faceless ghoul. A chilling creature that froze London with his unholy, merciless terror.

This bloody drama was played out to the full in one small area of the East End. Of the East End itself James Mackay wrote: '...it is the hell of poverty. Like an enormous black, motionless, giant Kraken, the poverty of London lies there in lurking silence and encircles with its mighty tentacles the life and wealth of the City and of the West End.' And of this area of grime and decay and hopelessness, the most wretched spot of all was Whitechapel. Jack London called it 'The Abyss'.

To starve on its streets was commonplace. To starve and die on its streets was unremarkable. And these filth-caked streets led to suffocating lanes and courtyards; and to even more sickening slimy-wastelands. There, in damp, mouldering houses were jam-packed the wretched of the earth; wretches who had lost every last shred of dignity and hope; wretches too drained, demoralized and apathetic to dream of raising the banner of revolt. They were doomed. Their heritage - a sunless day.

Into this setting came one man with a mission. He had no dream of uplift; he was no philanthropist; he had no message for the world. His mission was sordid beyond belief. He would take from the whores on those streets everything he craved. He would take their lives as an exercise in power. He would treat them like those specimens he had once carved up on mortuary slabs. It would be a brief reign of terror, but his memory would never die.

The women he chose to prey on were tragic, lost creatures. Not one of them had a fragment of allure. They justified the pity of anyone with a heart, but this heartless, fastidious man found their squalor an extra spur to his contempt. The women he came to terrorise were well pictured by a reporter from the *New York Herald*, who wrote:

NEW YORK HERALD

You can see them any evening, a dozen at least, on the pavement in front of the big old Spitalfields church. They are all over the adjacent district, but this is a sure place to find a group. They are old, actually or prematurely as the case may be. Their dress holds together but would not stand daylight. Their shoes are full of holes. Their bonnets would be rejected with nausea by a respectable rag-bag. They wear little, if any underclothing for several reasons, one of which is that it costs money. They are all bent, and walk slowly, the tottering gait of a wreck. And in all the scale of zoology there is nothing that can compare with the faces that look out at you in the flickering lights of the street.

They are seamed and seared and wrinkled and bloated. Their eyes are dull like those of dead fish... They are not vicious... Depravity is a feeble word, degradation a familiar and inadequate expression to describe their condition...

From the ranks of these tragic discards the victims would be drawn. The stalker had studied them for years. He knew just where to find his prey. Every street, alley and lane was known to him of old. He could even choose the very spots to leave them on display. He could straddle them across the giant map of Whitechapel that lay seared in his memory. *His* would be the kingdom, the power and the glory.

The Terror Begins

In 1888 two prostitutes were murdered in the back streets of Whitechapel, well before the Ripper struck, but no one thought of linking these killings to him. They were just two more of the brutalities that Whitechapel was long used to.

Then, prostitute Polly Nichols was found mutilated and disembowelled in Buck's Row, just opposite the London Hospital, and the picture changed dramatically.

Overnight the three killings were placed together. Now a pattern became observable; or so it seemed. But the observations were misguided; the Nichols murder was unconnected with the two earlier deaths. At the time only the killer knew that this murder was number one in a series that would dismay the civilized world. But in September 1888 belief that a single killer was responsible for all three deaths, dominated newspaper columns. The Star editorial for 1 September shows this well:

Have we a murderous maniac loose in East London? It looks as if we have. Nothing so appalling, so devilish, so inhuman - or, rather non-human - as the three Whitechapel crimes had ever happened outside the pages of Poe or De Quincey. The unravelled mystery of the 'Whitechapel Murders' would make a page of detective romance as ghastly as 'The Murders of the Rue Morgue'. The hellish violence and malignity of the crime which we described yesterday resemble in almost every particular the two other deeds of darkness which preceded it. Rational motive there appears to be none. The murderer must be a Man Monster...

And the account in the body of the paper spelled out the grim facts of the crime:

The victim of the latest Whitechapel horror - the woman who was found yesterday in Buck's Row completely disembowelled and with her head nearly gashed from her body – was identified as Mary Ann Nicholls, also tailed 'Polly Nicholls'....

There is a terribly SIGNIFICANT SIMILARITY between this ghastly crime and the two mysterious murders of women which have occurred in the same district within the last three months. In each ease the victim has been a woman of abandoned character, each crime has been committed in the dark hours of the morning, and more important still as pointing to one man, and that man a madman, being the culprit, each murder has been accompanied by hideous mutilation. In the second case, that of the woman Martha Turner, it will be remembered that no fewer than 30 stabs was inflicted. The scene of this murder was George-yard, a place appropriately known locally as 'the slaughter-house'. As in both other cases there was in this not the slightest clue to the murderer — no one was known to have any motive for causing the woman's death... The first murder, which, strangely enough, did not rouse much interest, was committed in Osborne Street. The woman in that case was alive when discovered, but unconscious, and she died in the hospital without recovering her senses, consequently she was unable to whisper a word to put the police on the track of her fiendish assailant, and her murder has remained a mystery. All three crimes have been committed WITHIN A VERY SMALL RADIUS. Each of the ill-lighted thoroughfares to which the women were decoyed to be foully butchered are off turnings from Whitechapel-road, and all are within half a mile. The fact that these three tragedies have been committed within such a limited area, and are so strangely alike in their details, is forcing on all minds the conviction that they are the work of some cool, cunning man with a mania for murder.

How right they were! In the safety of his retreat the real killer would have revelled in these words. But the police and the public would have no truck with the idea of a cool cunning man. The killer had to have hate written all over his face; his manner had to be menacing and evil. In that frame of mind they began to hunt for the man known as Leather Apron. If the gossip was true, then everyone seemed to know him. He was unmistakable, so they said. But who was he? And, more to the point, where was he?

Chapter 3

Maniac at Large?

While all the talk raged about Leather Apron, the second Ripper killing occurred in the backyard of No. 29 Hanbury Street, where John Davis found the body of Annie Chapman with her throat cut and her body mutilated. Her neck was slashed so deeply that the head was almost severed. She had been disembowelled. And there, near the butchered body of this second victim was thrown a leather apron.

Was it a taunt? Or had the killer left it behind in his haste? It was neither: the apron lay there after being cleaned outside under the yard tap. It belonged to John Richardson, whose mother lived at the place; so it had no significance whatsoever. Despite this, its discovery whipped up the fury against the strange,

LEFT The body of Annie Chapman, Jack the Ripper's second victim anonymous Jewish apron-wearer. This killing of 8 September convinced the Star that the time had come for popular action. Its leader on that day struck the keynote for its new campaign:

Two days after this appeal for vigilantes, the news broke that, at last, Leather Apron had been cornered and hauled into a police cell. His name was now known: he was John Pizer, a Jewish boot-finisher, of Mulberry Street, Whitechapel. Crude broadsheets soon reached the streets proclaiming the arrest of the prime suspect. The killer-Jew had been ensnared! The rope would soon stretch his loathsome *neck*. But it was otherwise. On 12 September the Pall Mall Gazette announced that Emanuel Violenia had witnessed a quarrel between a man and a woman in Hanbury Street. The man

> " There can be no shadow of a doubt now that our original theory was correct, and that the Whitechapel murderer, who has now four, if not five, victims to his knife, is one man, and that man a murderous maniac... "

had threatened to knife the woman and that man was believed to have been Pizer. An identification parade was held in the yard at Leman Street police station, with the result that:

> ....Violenia..... Having keenly scrutinised all the faces before him went up to Pizer and identified him as the man whom he heard threatens a woman on the night of the murder. Subsequently, cross-examination so discredited Violenia's evidence that it was wholly distrusted by the police, and Pizer was set at liberty.

Freedom for Pizer failed to satisfy the prejudiced, who were chained to the idea that the murders had to be the work of a 'low, dirty, foreign Jew'. No Britisher could sink to such depths. And while they seethed in their importance the real killer, every inch a scholarly English-

man, struck again; not once but twice; his third and fourth killings delivered in one night.

The first knifing came in Berner Street, but it was interrupted; no time for the ritual mutilations. The interrupted ritual was hateful to the killer's plans; he needed a second victim fast. With his nerves stretched to screaming point, strident police whistles adrenalized him. With killing time running out, he sped swiftly through the back streets to a new place of anguish - a place he knew - this time in the territory of the City of London Police, Mitre Square. A square patrolled every fifteen minutes by a City policeman. He had this short time only to entrap, kill and mutilate.

The *Star* for Monday 1 October paints part of the picture, but concentrates on the Berner Street murder, where witnesses seemed to have proliferated:

LEFT 29 Hanbury Street – the body of Annie Chapman was found in the back yard

The Star

Monday 1st October   1888

The first to find the body was Mr. Diemshitz, steward of the club. Interviewed by a Star reporter, Mr. Diemshitz said: - 'I was coming home from the market at one o'clock on Sunday morning... After I had passed through the gate...on driving into the yard my donkey shied a little in consequence of my cart coming in contact with something on the ground. On looking down I saw the ground was not level, so I took the butt end of my whip and touched what appeared to me in the dark to be a heap of dirt lately placed there, a thing I was not accustomed to see. Not being able to move it, I struck a match end and FOUND IT WAS A WOMAN. First of all I thought of my wife, but I found her inside the club enjoying herself with the others. I said to some of the members there is a woman lying in the yard, and I think she is drunk. Young Isaacs, a tailor machinist, went to the door and struck a match, and to our horror we saw blood trickling down the gutter almost from the fate to the club.......'

In the case of this murder, there was an eye-witness who claimed to have been in Berner Street and seen a struggle between the murder victim, Elizabeth Stride, and a man. This eye-witness was a Hungarian called Israel Schwartz. Through an interpreter he made a statement, first to the police, and then to a Star reporter, who ran him to earth in Backchurch Lane. According to his story, he had witnessed a quarrel between a half-tipsy man and a woman. This took place in the entrance to the alleyway where the body was later found. Schwartz made no attempt to intervene since a second man came out of the doorway of a public-house, yelled to the tipsy man and rushed towards Schwartz. On seeing a knife Schwartz fled from the scene.

A great deal has been made of this statement by Schwartz. It has been construed by some to be evidence that Schwartz was later able to identify the Ripper beyond doubt. At the time his statement was made, however, the Star maintained that 'the truth of the man's statement is not wholly acceptable.' This

" Catherine Eddowes murder in Mitre Square was the most sickening of all the killings up until then. Her intestines had been ripped from her body and thrown over one shoulder... "

clashes directly with Chief Inspector Swanson's verdict that there were no doubts about the honesty of Schwartz's statement.

There were similar claims to a sighting near to the spot where the second murder of that night took place. This was made by Joseph Lawende, who was walking past Mitre Square together with his friends Joseph Levy and Harry Harris. All three men saw a man and a woman talking there, but only Lawende was able to describe the man in any detail. These two 'sightings' have become part of a persistent myth that the Ripper himself was *definitely spotted* that night and later identified. Yet another myth grew out of that double event: the myth that the mutilations to victim Catherine Eddowes had been predicted in a letter to the Central News Agency.

Catherine Eddowes' murder in Mitre Square was the most sickening of all the

killings up until then. Her intestines had been ripped from her body and thrown over one shoulder, the left kidney and uterus had been knifed out of her and her face had been systematically disfigured. Her killer was still an anonymous fiend, but not for much longer. Within days the old cry of 'Leather Apron' was being replaced by a new one. An enterprising journalist had decided that the killer needed a memorable name, so he hit upon 'Jack the Ripper' and used it first in a letter then on a postcard.

He sent off his hoaxing letter on 27 September, promising in it: 'The next job I do I shall clip the lady's ears off...' This was followed by a postcard posted on 1 October regretting that: 'Couldn't finish straight off. Had no time to get ears for police...'

These hoaxes were published in the *Daily Telegraph* and this action led the *Star* (4 October) to lodge a protest:

Thursday 4th October **The Star** 1888

*B*y the way, why does our friend, the D.T., print facsimiles of the ghastly but very silly letters from 'Jack the Ripper'? We were offered them by the 'Central News', and declined to print them. They were clearly written in red pencil, not in blood, the obvious reason being that the writer was one of those foolish but bad people who delight in an unholy notoriety. Now, the murderer is not a man of this kind. His own love of publicity is tempered by a very peculiar and remarkable desire for privacy and by a singular ability to secure what he wants. Nor is there any proof of any pre-knowledge of the Mitre-square crimes, beyond the prediction that they were going to happen, which on body might have made. The reference to ear-clipping may be a curious coincidence, but there is nothing in the posting of the letter on Sunday. Thousands of Londoners had details of the crimes supplied in the Sunday papers.

Foolish or not, from then on everyone, including the *Star*, accepted that the name would inevitably be 'Jack the Ripper'. And the killer himself must have revelled in its gruesomeness. Then, while everyone was waiting for yet another knifing, the theorists began to refine their ideas. One such gentleman, a surgeon ill-received by the police, sought out the *Star* for help in promoting his views. Since these views were in line with those held by Archibald Forbes, the editor joined the two contributions together in a column on 6 October.

'*Clearly,*' said Mr. Forbes, '*the murderer is a man familiar with the geography of the Whitechapel purlieus. Clearly he is a man not unaccustomed in the manner of accosting these poor women as they are wont to be accosted. Clearly he is a man to whom the methods of the policemen are not unknown — the measured pace, the regular methodical round, the tendency to woodenness and unalertness of perception which are the characteristics of that well-meaning individual.*

'*Probably a dissolute man, he fell victim to a specific contagion, and so seri-*

ously that in the sequel he lost his career. What shape the deterioration may have taken, yet left him with a strong, steady hand, a brain of devilish coolness, and an active step, is not to be defined.

The man's physical health ruined,' continued Mr. Forbes, 'and his career broken, he has possibly suffered specific brain damage as well. At this moment - I cannot use exact professional terms — there may be mischief to one of the lobes of the brain. Or he may have become insane simply from anguish of body and distress of mind. Anyhow, he is mad, and his mania, rising from the particular to the general, takes the FELL FORM OF REVENGE against the class, a member of which has wrought: him his blighting hurt, against too, the persons of that class plying in Whitechapel, since it was from a Whitechapel loose woman that he took his scathe.'

Now this exactly describes the man whom the doctor suspects. He is a man of about 35: He was not a fully qualified surgeon, but had a certain amount of anatomical knowledge, and had assisted at operations, including ovariotomy. He was the assistant to a doctor in Whitechapel, and KNOWS EVERY ALLEY AND COURT in the neighbourhood of the places where the murders were committed. He has been the victim of 'a specific contagion,' and since then has been animated by feelings of hate, not to say revenge, against the lower class of women who haunt the streets...

In later years this published theory would also furnish material for a lasting myth. A myth so persuasive and attractive that Leonard Matters, author of the first book on the Ripper published in English, *The Mystery of Jack the Ripper*, actually based his 'solution' wholeheartedly on it. Matters used the basic formula of a doctor bent on revenge and created a totally fictitious 'Dr Stanley', to fill the bill. His Dr Stanley was presented as an authentic man who lived, breathed, loved, killed and made a death-bed confession. There was one major difference, however: it was the doctor's son who caught the venereal disease, and the distraught father who sought the revenge.

So, was any of the contemporary theories ever more than inspired guesswork? In truth few of them had any kind of merit. But the most stubborn, underlying theme of many of these theories was one of anti-Semitism - an idea which gained strength from the very nature of the mutilations.

Chapter 4

Confusion Grows

NEW
ority
Coron
hird

RIGHT The house to house searches fell heaviest on the Jewish population. Few believed that the murderer could be English. It was much easier to assume he was "foreign"

Certain parts of some of the victims had been taken away, that much the public knew. It soon became known that the uterus had been removed from the scene in at least two cases. This was gruesome enough but then even more gruesome stories came in from the Continent suggesting a bizarre use for the missing organs. The Star ran one of these stories on 9 October 1888, which read in part:

.....certain facts.... may throw a new light on the Whitechapel murders. In various German criminal codes...punishments are prescribed for the mutilation of female corpses, with the object of making from the uterus and other organs 'thieves' candles' or 'soporific candles'.

According to an old superstition, still rife in various parts of Germany, the light from such candles will throw those upon whom it falls into the deepest slumbers, and they may, consequently, become a valuable instrument to the thieving profession...

When a similar account ran in *Police News* it was supplemented with a piece which said that such loathsome candles had also been introduced into the evidence at the trial of the Jew, Moses Ritter, a continental case of much bitterness.

Such words were honey to those who wished to fix the killings on the Jews. These people were sure to have been smugly satisfied by the news printed by the *Star* on 17 October:

Thursday 17th October

The Star

1888

Whitechapel
A House to House Search Among the Jews

*T*he police are making a house to house visit amongst the Jews at the East-End. They demand admission to every room, look underneath the beds, and peer into the smallest cupboards. They ask for the production of knives, and examine them. In some cases they have been refused admittance until proof was produced of authority...

Adding to this anti-Semitism was the persistent chatter about a mysterious message left by the Ripper in Goulston Street just after the Mitre Square murder. It was something like 'the Jews not being blamed for nothing', or perhaps 'the Juwes not being blamed'; there was no certainty among the rumour mongers. Perhaps this was the fault of the police high-command. The writing had been rubbed out by order of Commissioner of Police Sir Charles Warren. Not even a photograph of the message had been allowed.

This growing hostility against the Jews was increased by a malicious story telegraphed to *The Times* from Vienna. The story alleged that the *Talmud* specifically sanctioned the mutilation by Jews of Gentile women. The Chief Rabbi, Dr Hermann Adler, wrote a bitter protest on reading this gross calumny:

CONFUSION GROWS

...Many English and Irish workpeople in the East End are inflamed against the immigrant Jews by the competition for work and houses, by the stories of the sweaters and the sweated. If these illogical and ignorant minds should come to believe in the report heedlessly spread by a writer who is not quite just nor well informed himself, the results might be terrible.

Dr Adler's protest had little effect. The Jews were an easy target; they looked different; they ate differently; they spoke differently; and they were saddled with the collective responsibility for the death of Christ. Even the usually radical *Pall Mall Gazette* fell into the trap of using continental stories that reflected badly on the Jews. This led to a sorrowful letter from Samuel Montagu, the Jewish MP for Whitechapel:

Being a constant reader and in general accord with your policy of defending the weak against the strong, I felt much pain in reading in your yesterday's issue gave insinuations against the Jews who live in my constituency. In Jewish history there are frequent records that, when epidemics have occurred, or murders have taken place, false accusations have been made against the Jews, inciting the ignorant and the criminal classes of acts of violence. In this enlightened country, with an educated working class, no such fear need be entertained; but why recall the red spectre of bygone ages when religious persecution was a matter of course, whichever Christian creed was in power?

Few have greater experience than I of the Jew of this and of other countries, thus I am able to say with confidence that no similar class of human beings is as free from acts of violence as the Jews of Europe and America.

You may be right in blaming the authorities for not preserving a facsimile of the chalk inscription, which would have dispelled any chance of accusation against the Jews, although I cannot see how the atrocious acts of one man should affect a class. It has been generally admitted that the murderer had considerable practical knowledge of anatomy, and I do not believe that there exists such an individual among the Jews of East London. If the 'handwriting on the wall' was done by the monster himself, can there be any doubt of his intentions to throw the pursuers on a wrong track while showing hostility to the Jews in the vicinity.

Once again it is doubtful if these words of caution had any real effect. It is true that on one accused a specific Jewish doctor, but with 'Jewish wall writings', and Jewish corpse-candles' in the public mind, it was inevitable that someone would hint that a Jewish ritual-slaughter man, or *shochet*, could be at work.

For a time the police actually took this seriously and checked on the men practiced in *shechita* butchery. While all these futile diversions were taking up time and energy, the Ripper made his last foray, and made it the most spectacular of all.

❝ It has been generally admitted that the murderer had considerable practical knowledge of anatomy, and I do not believe that there exists such an individual among the Jews of East London ❞

Chapter 5

The Bloody Pinnacle

The Ripper chose the one day when all eyes would be centred on the City: the ninth day of November; Lord Mayor's Day. As the gilded coach stood waiting for the great procession, only a handful of people knew that the day would be completely dominated and overshadowed by the mocking killer.

Just a short distance away, in a shambles of a room, lay the most mutilated of all the victims. Mary Kelly had been unwise enough to usher the killer into her sordid bedroom. For the first time the Ripper had access to an improvised operating theatre. Every unexplored ritual could be carried out without haste or fear of interruption. *Police News* ran a report designed to sicken anyone who read it:

The victim was another of the unfortunate class, who occupied a miserably furnished room in a court off Dorset-street, a narrow thoroughfare out of Commercial-street... Such a shocking state of things was there as has probably never been equalled in the annals of crime. The throat had been cut right across with a knife, nearly severing the head from the body. The abdomen had been ripped partially open, and both of the breasts had been cut from the body. The left arm, like the head, hung to the body by the skin only. The nose had been cut off, the forehead skinned, and the thighs, down to the feet, stripped of the flesh. The abdomen had been slashed with a knife across and downwards, and the liver and entrails wrenched away. The entrails and other portions of the frame were missing, but the liver, etc, it is said, were found placed between the feet of this poor victim. The flesh from the thighs and legs, together with the breasts and nose, had been placed by the murderer on the table, and one of the hands of the dead woman had been pushed into her stomach.

The first cries of horror from the newsboys cut through the cheering as Lord Mayor Whitehead drew near to St Paul's. All the gilt splendour failed to eclipse the black news from the East End.

Within days, the hysteria on the Whitechapel streets reached new heights. On 11 November, a crowd seized a Ripper suspect and cries of 'Lynch him!' were heard. Only swift action by the police prevented the man from being seriously injured. On 15 November, a City policeman in civilian clothes was surrounded by a small mob yelling that he was the Ripper. Within seconds the crowds had grown from dozens to hundreds, and escape was impossible. Once again, it was only the timely intervention by police constables that saved the

man. And on the same day, one arrest caused more than usual excitement. As *The Times* reports:

The Times

A man stared into the face of a woman in the Whitechapel Road and she at once screamed out that he was 'Jack the Ripper'. The man was immediately surrounded by an excited and threatening crowd, from which he was rescued with some difficulty by the police. He was then taken under a strong escort to the Commercial Street Police Station, followed by an enormous mob of men and women shouting and screaming at him in the most extraordinary manner. At the police station the man proved to be a German... He explained through an interpreter that he arrived in London from Germany on Tuesday and was to leave for America today.

At this turbulent time the Metropolitan police were shaken by the news that their Chief Commissioner, Sir Charles Warren, had resigned. His running battle with the Home Secretary, Charles Matthews, was over. An article by Warren in *Murrays Magazine* had contained too many indiscretions to be ignored and the two men met in a head-on clash. Resignation was Warren's only way of making one last protest, but few admired his stand; many in fact rejoiced in his downfall.

But was the hunt for the killer improved by this dramatic change at the top? If we judge by the results, then it made not the slightest difference, and as the year drew to its close nothing but false trails were explored. But did the police really have no clues to guide them? Well, they did have one incredibly detailed description of the man 'last seen with Kelly on the night of her death.

This 'eye-witness' report counts as a classic in its own right. It is quite unbelievably detailed since the observation was conducted in the murk of a gas-lit street. Nevertheless this report was taken seriously, especially by the popular press. The Star ran the description on 14 November:

The story is told by George Hutchinson.... He says: - '...about two o'clock on Friday morning....I came down Whitechapel road into Commercial-street. As I passed Thrawl Street I saw a man standing at the corner of the street, and as I went towards Flower and Dean- street I met the woman Kelly, whom I knew very well, having been in her company a number of times. She said, "Mr. Hutchinson, can you lend me sixpence?" I said, "I cannot, as I am spent out going down to Romford." She then walked on towards Thrawl street, saying, "I must go and look for some money." The man who was standing at the corner of Thrawl-street came towards her and PUT HIS HAND ON HER SHOULDER and said something to her, which I did not hear, and they both burst out laughing. He put his hand again on her shoulder, and they both walked slowly towards me. I walked on to the corner of Fashion-street, near the public-house. As they came by me his arm was still on her shoulder. Fie had a soft felt hat on, and this was drawn down somewhat over his eyes. I put down my head to look him in the face, and he turned and looked at me very sternly, and they walked across the road to Dorset-street. I followed them across, and stood at the corner of Dorset-street. They stood at the corner of Miller s-court for about three minutes. Kelly spoke to the man in a loud voice, saying, "I have lost my handkerchief." He pulled a RED HANDKERCHIEF out of his pocket, and gave it to Kelly, and they both went up the court together. I went to look up the court to see if I could see them, but could not. I stood there for three-quarters of an hour to see if they came down again, but they did not, and so I went away. My suspicions were aroused by seeing the man so well-dressed, but I had no suspicion that he was the murderer. The man was about 5ft. 6in. in height, and 34 or 35 years of age, with dark complexion and dark moustache, turned up at the ends. He was wearing a long dark coat, trimmed with astrakhan, a white collar, with black necktie, in which was affixed a horseshoe pin. He wore a pair of dark 'spats' with light buttons over button boots, and displayed from his waistcoat a massive gold chain. His watch chain had a big seal, with a red stone, hanging from it. He had a heavy moustache curled up and dark eyes and bushy eyebrows. He had no side whiskers, and his chin was clean-shaven. He LOOKED LIKE A FOREIGNER....'

This pen-portrait soon became transformed into an 'artist's impression' that featured on the front-page in the 24 November Police News and influenced the public vision of the killer. Over the years the features depicted in this artist's wood-engraving have been positively identified as those of Walter Sickert; Fredrick Deeming; George Chapman; Neill Cream; Pedachenko; Eddy, Duke of Clarence; Sir Randolph Churchill and James Maybrick!

After Kelly's murder Police News published this map and added to the confusion since only the last five were genuine Ripper murders.

MAP OF THE WHITECHAPEL MURDERS

1. **Emma Smith**
2. **Martha Turner**
3. **Mary Ann Nichols**
4. **Annie Chapman**
5. **Elizabeth Stride**
6. **Catherine Eddowes**
7. **Mary Kel**

Chapter 6

The Year Ends, The Fears Remain

Given that good clues were elusive, one event on 19 December seemed to throw a new light on the killer's methods. It all began with the finding of a dead woman in Poplar; a woman later named as Rose Mylett.

Sensational reports at the time said that the dead woman's throat bore the unmistakable white mark of a strangler's cord. Despite this she was still a victim of Jack the Ripper! This strange conclusion resulted from some ideas put forward by Dr Matthew Brownfield, the police surgeon at Poplar. He was of the opinion that the Ripper victims were all first strangled by a cord because this rendered them unconscious and gave the killer the chance to cut their throats so much more cleanly and deliberately.

By cutting the throat along the line of the cord he would obliterate all traces of partial strangulation, and add to the mystery. Evidence that the mark on her throat had been caused by too tight a collar was obviously dismissed with scorn by the inquest jury who decided it was murder. But in his autobiography Sir Robert Anderson (one-time Head of the CID) swept aside the jury's verdict of 'Murder by person or persons unknown' and wrote: 'The Poplar case of December, 1888, was death from natural causes, and but for the "Jack the Ripper" scare, no one would have thought of suggesting that it was homicide.'

Whether he was right or wrong is of little account. The murders hail ended with the death of Kelly. No one but the Ripper knew that the killings had stopped (if only for the time being); but everyone was still waiting for the next outrage, so naturally, any type of attack on the 'unfortunates' in the East End was enough to raise the cry of 'The Ripper'. This is exactly what happened in 1889.

The first Ripper scare of 1889 erupted on 17 July, when the body of Alice McKenzie was found in Whitechapel's Castle Alley. Her throat was cut and her abdomen seemed to be gashed. But Dr Bagster Phillips soon ruled her out as one of his victim's. The abdominal wounds were superficial, not the extensive slashes favoured by Jack. And the throat had been cut with a short-bladed knife, very different from the long blades used by the Ripper. The press was not impressed; this had to be another Ripper job, and they were determined to stress the point. Their readers went on believing them and when a second body was discovered under a railway arch this simply showed that the press was right. But this second corpse, dumped just off Backchurch lane, was headless and legless. The woman in this case had been dead for some days; all the cuts had been made cleanly and with decision; there was not the slightest hint of frenzy. It could well have been the work of some leisurely medical student. There was

nothing to connect it with the killings of 1888.

Only one more pseudo Ripper murder gained wide coverage. On 13 February 1891 a prostitute names Frances Coles was found slashed and ripped under a railway arch off Royal Mint Street. There was still a small spark of life left when she was found, so the killer must have darted off just seconds before the police arrived. Search parties were organised within minutes and the area was sealed off, but all the efforts were in vain.

A lead to the possible killer came from Coles' lodgings. A man with a bleeding hand had called looking for her. He had spun a yarn about being robbed and injured, and then he went off to find a hospital. The tale sounded suspicious; could this be the Ripper at last? The man was swiftly traced and identified. He was James Saddler, a ship's fireman, who not only knew Frances but had even bought her a hat the day before.

For a while the case against him looked firm and he was arrested and charged with murder. But the Stokers' Union came to his aid. Their solicitor Harry Wilson, demolished, bit by bit, the case for the prosecution. Finally, in the interests of justice the Attorney-General decided that the case had to be

Sir Arthur Conan Doyle – the creator of Sherlock Holmes – did he meet the Ripper?

dropped. With that Saddler slunk out of the limelight and the last great Ripper scare petered out. But theories about the Ripper went on multiplying.

He was now abroad, said some, and stories from both Nicaragua and Jamaica lent support to their claims. In both those places prostitutes had been slain and mutilated by an unknown killer; in Managua six women had been butchered in less than ten days. Whether these horrors were inspired by reports about the London murders is an open question, but they were found to be unconnected with the man known as Jack.

Many of the other theories make strange reading. And there are famous names among the theorists; names like William Morris, Walter Crane, George Moore, Bernard Shaw, and other socially minded thinkers of the period. A whole book could be made up from these musings alone. Reading them one is struck with the thought that some of these men may well have known the Ripper and never once suspected him. For at one time he moved in the same circles as Bernard Shaw and even Conan Doyle, without being named by either of them. Did the creator of Sherlock Holmes ever have the faintest idea that the quarry was nigh? And were the police any brighter?

Chapter 7

Fairy Tales?

Until 1910 the only published clues to the main police suspects were contained in the short account given by Major Arthur Griffiths in his Mysteries of Police and Crime. He confirmed that the police had suspected:

…several persons, all of them known to be homicidal lunatics. Against three of these they held very plausible and reasonable grounds of suspicion... One was a Polish Jew, a known lunatic, who was at large in the district of Whitechapel at the time of the murders, and who, having developed homicidal tendencies, was afterwards confined in an asylum. The second possible criminal was a Russian doctor, also insane... The third person was of the same type, but the suspicion in his case was stronger... He also was a doctor in the prime of life, was believed to be insane or on the borderland of insanity... On the last day of that year (1888) his body was found floating in the Thames, and was said to have been in the water a month. The theory was that... his brain entirely gave way, and he became furiously insane and committed suicide.

No priority is given in this account to any one of the three candidates. This state of limbo changed when Sir Robert Anderson wrote his memoirs. The first version of the significant part of these memoirs appeared in the March 1910 issue of *Blackwood's Magazine*. This was followed soon afterwards by book publication under the title *The Lighter Side of My Official Life*. His comments on the identity of the killer led to a frosty rebuke from Sir Henry Smith, late of the City Police, and to two further objections: one from a City of London solicitor, George Kebbell; the other from the well- known 'expert in lunacy' Dr Forbes Winslow. These are Anderson's words that caused the furore:

> One did not need to be a Sherlock Holmes to discover that the criminal was a sexual maniac of a virulent type; that he was living in the immediate vicinity of the scenes of the murders; and that, if he was not living absolutely alone, his people knew his guilt, and refused to give him up to justice. I luring my absence abroad the Police had made a house-to-house search for him, investigating the case of every man in the district whose circumstances were such that he could go and come and get rid of his blood-stains in secret. And the conclusion we came to was that he and his people were certain low-class Polish Jews; for it is a remarkable fact that people of that class in the East End will not give up one of their number to justice.
>
> And the result proved that our diagnosis was right on every point. For I may say at once that 'undiscovered murders' are rare in London and the 'Jack-the-Ripper' crimes are not within the category...I will only add here that the 'Jack-the-Ripper' letter which is preserved in the Police Museum at New Scotland Yard is the creation of an enterprising London journalist.
>
> Having regard to the interest attaching to the case, I am almost tempted to disclose the identity of the murderer and the pressman who wrote the letter above referred to. But no public benefit would result from such a course, and the traditions of my old department would suffer. I will merely add that the only person who ever saw the murderer unhesitatingly identified the suspect the instant he was confronted with him; but he refused to give evidence against him.
>
> In saying that he was a Polish Jew I am merely stating a definite ascertained fact. And my words are meant to specify race, not religion. For it would outrage all religious sentiment to talk of the religion of a loathsome creature whose utterly unmentionable vices reduced him to a lower level than that of a brute.

Major Smith's rebuke prompted no visible activity, but solicitor Kebbell's comments provoked an appeal to a Magistrate at the Bow Street Court. A report of these proceedings was carried by the Umpire on Sunday 31 July. In part, it ran:

WHO WAS JACK-THE-RIPPER?

ENGLISH SHERLOCK HOLMES ON THE MANIAC'S IDENTITY

*A*gain the identity of the notorious murderer who called himself Jack-the-Ripper has cropped up. This time a lady living in Melbourne writes to Dr. Forbes Winslow, the Sherlock Holmes of these East End murders, and asserts that the fellow is a native of Melbourne, a college graduate, was called 'Jack', always carried an ugly sheath knife, and had told her that he was the perpetrator of the frightful series of crimes.

Quite recently the controversy was reopened by Sir Robert Anderson, formerly head of Scotland Yard, who contended that the miscreant was a Jew and that he was not arrested because the only man who could identify him was a co-religionist who refused to speak.

Mr. George Kebbell, a City of London solicitor, controverted this by declaring that Sir Robert was entirely in the wrong in that 'Jack-the-Ripper' was an Irishman who had been a medical student but had sinned, had been cast out by his family and had descended in the social scale until he became a casual fireman on board a cattle boat. Mr. Kebbell declared that this man, just after the Whitechapel murders, was caught in the very act of mutilating a woman, who, by a miracle, escaped death and gave evidence against him. The fellow was sentenced to ten years' penal servitude...

Dr. Forbes Winslow spent many days and nights hunting for the 'ripper', and, as a result, he asked Mr. Marsham, the Bow-street magistrate, to advise him as to what could be done in the case of the Irish medical student, who, in February, 1895, was sentenced to ten years' penal servitude for wounding a woman in Whitechapel.

Proceeding, Dr. Forbes Winslow said that while the student was serving that sentence statements were made, prompted probably by the nature of the offence, of which he said he was innocent, that he was none other than 'Jack-the-Ripper'.

In court Dr. Forbes Winslow said: 'I knew that there was no foundation for these statements, and I took up the man's case. A few days ago I received a letter from a lady in Australia. The object she had in writing this letter to me was to clear the Irish medical student I have referred to from the accusation that he committed these murders. This lady was acquainted with a man who left England in 1889, the last year in which these murders were committed.

FAIRY TALES?

He went to Australia, and the lady became engaged to him there; but from certain facts which came to her knowledge, and from a confession made, she concluded that he was none other than "Jack-the-Ripper."...she is convinced in her own mind, that the real "Jack-the-Ripper" was the man who went to Australia, and who is at the present moment working in South Africa.

Speaking of the various attempts to identify Jack-the-Ripper, Dr. Winslow remarked to a special representative of the Umpire: 'Of the many people who saw and spoke to the unknown murderer, there came never a suggestion that he was either a Jew or an Irishman.

Again, I should say that Mr. Kebbell is mistaken his man for several reasons. To begin with, if he noticed that the man he defended before the magistrates was an Irishman, then some of my informants would have noticed it also. Now, I traced Jack-the-Ripper from one lodging to another, and all my first-hand descriptions fail to tally with Mr. Kebbell's in every way.

'I am convinced that the murderer of the eight unfortunates during 1888 and 1889 was an epileptic maniac, a man who at times was a homicidal maniac and at other times was quite sane.

'At the time of the crimes I threw my whole heart and soul into the subject, and I am still of the same mind - that Jack-the-Ripper was an Englishman, probably thirty-five years of age; that he was well educated, and had studied surgery in his earlier days. His conversation was often quite above the heads of his hearers, and he would talk by the hour on the morality of people.

'I have no doubt that when seized by homicidal mania he believed that he had a mission to perform, namely, to strike such a blow at open immorality that women would henceforth not dare to parade their vices... So well-known was my association with the hunt for Jack-the-Ripper that he actually wrote to me. These two epistles are, I firmly believe, genuine, because the writing corresponds with various inscriptions chalked under Whitechapel arches, while on one occasion he sent me the date on which he would commit his next outrage, and he kept his word, even though I had given notice to the police. This crime was carried out on Lord Mayor's day, and while the crowd was at its thickest to view the show newsboys were crying in the streets, "Another Whitechapel Murder!"...

'If the police will co-operate with me,' concluded Dr. Winslow, "Jack-the-Ripper" can be safe in prison in London in six months' time. I should be prepared to go out myself with a policeman and fetch him.'

Dr. Lyttleton Forbes Winslow came from a family of asylum owners, and had given expert testimony in criminal cases, so his views seemed to have some weight behind them. In fact at the time of the murders he was regarded as an outstanding authority on the real personality of the Ripper. Of his own powers he had no doubt. He even wrote:

> *Day after day and night after night I spent in the Whitechapel slums. The detectives knew me, the lodging housekeepers knew me, and at last the poor creatures of the street came to know me. In terror they rushed to me with every scrap of information which might to my mind be of value. To me the frightened women looked for hope. In my presence they felt reassured and welcomed me to their dens and obeyed my commands eagerly, and found bits of information I wanted.*

Who could possibly dismiss such a worthy fellow as a humbug and a fantasist and a liar? But that is what he was. His claim to have warned the Yard *before* the Kelly murder is false. The letter he later produced to try to prove his claim can be shown to have had its date altered. It was originally dated 19 October 1889, and was one of a spate of such letters sent at that time. But the year has been crudely altered to read '1888'. And a thoughtful examination of the text confirms that it is based on events of 1889 beyond doubt. Thus at least two of Anderson's protagonists are not to be taken seriously. Major Smith, by contrast, had a valid point when he said: Surely Sir Robert cannot believe that while the Jews, as he asserts, were entering into this conspiracy to defeat the ends of justice, there was no one among them with sufficient knowledge of the criminal law to warn them of the risks they were running?'

But, despite Major Smith's objections, could Anderson possibly have truth on his side?

> " If the police will co-operate with me, concluded Dr. Winslow, Jack-the-Ripper can be safe in prison in London in six months time "

Chapter 8

The Riddles of Zion

Anderson's Polish Jew remained anonymous until a few years ago when writer, Martin Fido, began to look at this neglected man. He reasoned that Anderson had been writing about Kosminski, one of the three listed by Macnaghten. This may seem an obvious linkage but Don Rumbelow, for one, had earlier concluded, '... it seems abundantly clear that Anderson was accusing John Pizer (Leather Apron) of being the Ripper'. But Martin Fido was certain that only one man fitted Anderson's description, and he began searching through the records of public asylums and workhouse infirmaries. His diligence paid off. In the records of admissions for Colney Hatch Asylum he found an entry for Aaron Kosminski. Was this the man he

was hunting for? Unfortunately for his theory this Kosminski was not taken in until 6 February 1891. This simply failed to match. The man indicated by Anderson had to have been inside an asylum in March 1889. In addition lunatic Aaron was simply a poor wretch suffering from delusions; a sad figure impelled to search for bread in the gutters of the streets. Fido came to the reluctant conclusion that: '...with eighteen months of harmless scavenging from the gutters from 1888 to 1890, Kosminski could not have been the Ripper.'

A revised theory had to be quickly evolved. Perhaps there had been a confusion of names at some point? Maybe the killer had been penned up under a name quite like Kosminski? From that

> "...with eighteen months of harmless scavenging from the gutters from 1888 to 1890, Kosminski could not have been the Ripper"

point Martin Fido made a fresh search and came up with Nathan Kaminsky, a Polish Jew who on 24 March 1888, began a six-week course of treatment for syphilis at the Whitechapel Workhouse Infirmary. After that the records were bare. No trace of the man anywhere. Fido met this challenge by theorizing that Kaminsky had been incarcerated under some other name and then concluded that a Colney Hatch patient logged as David Cohen was identical with the missing Kaminsky. Cohen had been brought in on 21 December 1888 and had died there on 20 October 1889. He was an extremely violent man more often found in a strait-jacket than without. He was also, in Fido's view, unmistakably Anderson's Polish Jew. In other words, Jack the Ripper.

It was a theory that was in dire trouble within weeks of its first appearance. On 19 October 1987 the *Daily Telegraph* published some notes made by Chief Inspector Donald Swanson in 1910. These had been jotted down on the pages of his copy of Anderson's autobiography, and at the point where Anderson states that the murderer had been identified by a man who refused to testify against him, Swanson wrote: 'because the suspect was also a Jew and also because his evidence would convict the suspect, and witness would be the means of the murderer being hanged which he did not wish to be left on his mind. And after this identification, no other murder of this kind took place in London.'

On the end paper of the book Swanson wrote a most remarkable observation. It is badly worded, but its meaning is clear:

> ...*after the suspect had been identified at the Seaside Home where he had been sent by us with difficulty in order to subject him to identification, and he knew he was identified. On suspect's return to his brother's house in Whitechapel he was watched by police (City CID) by day and night. In a very short time the suspect with his hands tied behind his back, was sent to Stepney Workhouse and then to Colney Hatch and died shortly afterwards - Kosminsky was the suspect.*

RIGHT Chief inspector Donald Swanson - Swanson was in overall charge of the investigation into murders from 1 September to 6 October 1888

Swanson puts no dates on record, but the Seaside Home he mentions was the Police Convalescent Home at Brighton, which only opened in March 1890. By that time David Cohen was dead and buried. Apart from that, Cohen had no next-of-kin, hence no 'brother's house' to return to. Martin Fido's Ripper Cohen is patently not the same as Swanson's Ripper Kosminski. Despite that, Fido has gone on record saying: 'I am quite convinced that he [Swanson] confirms my thesis that Aaron Kosminksi who lived at "his brother's house" in Whitechapel was somehow confused with David Cohen, who probably committed the Whitechapel Murders...'

So, was the original yarn about Kosminski simply an idea that Swanson came to nurse and passed on to Anderson? Did it get garbled in the same way that many of the police reminiscences became garbled? Major Smith, for a start, was wildly inaccurate at times. So was Macnaghten. And in the case of Inspector Reid we have his absurd statements that the Ripper only left '...a number of slashes all over the body of the victim, even after the murderer knew his victim was dead (and) at no time was any part of the body

missing.' He also believed that the Ripper had nine victims!

Did the police, then, have any certain evidence that allowed them to make a solid, sober, definitive identification? Do the existing records persuade us to trust Anderson on this score?

Chapter 9

Without a Clue

Anderson has been regarded as inaccurate and dogmatic by several historians. It can be argued that anyone whose thinking has been governed by fundamentalism of any sort: religious, political, scientific, rigid dogmatism always stands in the way of clear thinking. It promotes a feeling of certainty where caution should rule. For that reason, was Anderson simply repeating the truth as he had come to see it?

But this is not objective, historical truth. His writings are not those of someone possessing real knowledge - that is why they are so sketchy. At no point does he say 'I was there when the identification was made.' He is trading in second-hand information, and yet the solution to the great mystery would have dragged any sensible

police chief from one end of the country to the other. So what did he really know?

Some have argued that a crucial sighting of the Ripper was made on the night of the double event. One group favours the sighting by Schwartz at Berner Street, another opts for Lawende's sighting near Mitre Square. One of these eyewitnesses, so the reasoning runs, was much later able to finger Kosminski.

Let us spell out what this implies: on 30 September the police knew for certain that the murderer had been seen, beyond doubt. They knew, as well, that they had testimony from a person who could pick out the killer without hesitation. In short they had an invaluable clue in their hands and needed a face-to-face confrontation between their witness and the killer to tie the whole

> **"A crime of this kind should have been committed without any clue being supplied by the criminal is unusual"**

case up. Is this at all possible? Anderson's own words prove this to be absurd. Consider first of all his report to the Home Secretary on 23 October 1888. The telling part reads:

> I wish to guard against its being supposed that the inquiry is now concluded. There is no reason for furnishing these reports at this moment except that they have been called for.
>
> That a crime of this kind should have been committed without any clue being supplied by the criminal is unusual, but that five successive murders should have been committed, without our having the slightest clue of any kind is extraordinary, if not unique, in the annals of crime. The result has been to necessitate our giving attention to innumerable suggestions, such as would in any ordinary case be dismissed unnoticed, and no hint of any kind, which was not obviously absurd, has been neglected.

Does it really have to be hammered home that this alone destroys the fallacy that a key witness was known? Perhaps it does need hammering, since the significance of these words seem to have been missed by too many people. Very well, the man is confessing without reservations that he does not have *'the slightest clue of any kind'*. No witnesses; no trails leading to a hideout; no bloody clothing that can be fitted to a suspect; nothing. And years later Anderson confirmed that they had been without clues and that their efforts had resulted in 'non-detection'. His admissions came in a front-page interview given by him to the *Daily Chronicle*, on 1 September 1908. It was an interview prompted by the Luard case and Anderson first compared the British police procedures with those of the French - to the detriment of the British. In France, he argued, a tight control would be exercised over access to crime-sites. Clues would be protected from destruction by this control. Not so in Britain. He then went on:

1st September 1908

Daily Chronicle

*S*omething of the same kind happened in the Ripper crimes. In two cases of that series there were distinct clues destroyed - wiped out absolutely - clues that might very easily have secured for us proof of the identity of the assassin. In one case it was a clay pipe. Before we could get to the scene of the murder the doctor had taken it up, thrown it into the fireplace and smashed it beyond recognition. In another case there was writing in chalk on the wall - a most valuable clue; handwriting that might have been recognised at once as belonging to a certain individual, but before we could secure a copy, or get it protected, it had been obliterated... I told Sir William Harcourt, who was then Home Secretary, that I could not accept responsibility for the non-detection of the author of the Ripper crimes, for the reasons, among others, that I have given you...

Since the police were so baffled, they inevitably had free scope to develop individual theories. In time, these theories became hardened into certainties. But, with hindsight, we can see that they were all based on a hopelessly inadequate store of knowledge. They had not the dimmest vision of the person they should have been looking for. Some of them actually knew the killer, but never suspected him. They would have recognized him as the killer, only if they had found him standing over a corpse, ritually carving away.

Chapter 10

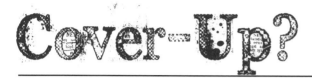

Cover-Up?

RIGHT Sir Melville Macnaghten, Chief Commissioner of the Metropolitan Police, named his three prime Ripper suspects in order to deflect the accusation of a cover-up involving the lunatic nephew of a high-ranking police officer

Since 1965 all serious research into the police suspects has been inspired by an odd document penned by Commissioner of Police Melville Macnaghten. This lengthy document is dated 23 February 1894 and in it he names three men as his prime suspects. But why bother to go to such lengths at that time? The murders had long since ceased and no spiky Home Secretary was pressing for quick answers. The truth is that his need to write was forced on him by outside pressure from the newspaper world.

It all began with a whisper conveyed to a reporter on the *Sun*. A patient held behind bars at Broadmoor Asylum was believed to be none other than the Ripper, but his connection with those murders had been hushed up. This was enough for the newspaper to mount an investigation and by 13 February 1894 the *Sun* presses were ready to roll off the first instalment of their great scoop. It took five days to tell the whole story and after the sensation had animated enough interest, the editor, Member of Parliament, T. P. O'Connor, decided that an editorial was called for. It appeared on 19 February:

Slowly, but steadily, the public has come to the same conclusion as that to which we have been forced by months of investigation - that in the witless wretch who is at present in Broadmoor Lunatic Asylum we have traced the author of the Whitechapel murders. We are not surprised that our statement should at first have been received with a certain degree of incredulity...

What reserve we had to make to defeat the arts of rivals, we were bound still further to increase by our sense of public welfare and our desire to spare feeling. Many correspondents have written to us to demand that we should give the name of 'Jack the Ripper' to the public. We may have to do so in the end, but we shall do so unwillingly, for it is hard to make the innocent suffer for the guilty, and to expose the unhappy relatives - if such there will be - to the reprobation which will gather around his name. But we shall send to the police, when they ask for it, all the material at our disposal. The names which we had in veil under initials will be revealed to them. We have likewise the addresses, the occupations, all the particulars, with regard to all the persons who can either entirely reveal or throw considerable light on the mystery we claim to have solved. We understand that the attention of the highest police authorities has been called to our statements, and we confidently look forward to our story being subjected to the closest and most searching investigation. We believe that with others, as with us, facts will point irresistibly to the conclusion that the man we point out is undoubtedly the long-sought criminal.

Macnaghten was alerted and alarmed by the suggestion that the *Sun* would name the inmate. He already knew about the man held in Broadmoor and he sensed trouble if the name was made public, since it would not take long for people to discover that inmate Cutbush was the nephew of Executive Superintendent Charles Henry Cutbush, of Scotland Yard. A grave risk presented itself: the risk of an outcry fanned by a hostile press. The charge would inevitably be 'cover-up by the police, for the police'. It was an outcome that Macnaghten dreaded. So, as a precaution Macnaghten prepared a statement and filed it at the Yard. There it laid, potential ammunition for his underlings in the event of a disclosure. Though marked 'Confidential', it was never meant to be a secret document - only the names were meant to be kept under wraps. Indeed, this document was carefully leaked to friendly outsiders like Major Arthur Griffiths. Its full text reads:

CONFIDENTIAL

*T*he case referred to in the sensational story in 'The Sun in its issue of 13th inst, & following dates, is that of Thomas Cutbush who was arraigned at the London County Sessions in April 1891, on a charge of maliciously wounding Florence Grace Johnson, and attempting to wound Isabelle Frazer Anderson in Kennington. He was found to be insane and sentenced to be detained during Her Majesty's pleasure.

This Cutbush, who lived with his mother and aunt at 14 Albert St. Kennington, escaped from the Lambeth Infirmary, (after he had been detained there only a few hours, as a lunatic) at noon on 5 March 1891. He was arrested on the 9th idem. A few weeks before this, several cases of stabbing, or jabbing from behind hail occurred in the vicinity, and a man named Colicutt was arrested, but subsequently discharged owing to faulty identification. The cuts in the girls' dresses made by Colicutt were quite different to the cut made by Cutbush (when he wounded Miss Johnson) who was no doubt influenced by a wild desire of morbid imitation. Cutbush's antecedents were enquired into by Ch. Insp.(now Supt.) [unreadable], by Insp. Race, and by R S. McCarthy C.I.D. (the last named officer had been specially employed in Whitechapel at the time of the mur-

ders there) and it was ascertained that he was born, and had lived in Kennington all his life. His father died when he was quite young, and he was always a 'spoilt' child. He had been employed as a clerk and traveller in the Tea trade at the Minories, & subsequently canvassed for a Directory in the East End, during which time he bore a good character. He apparently contracted syphilis about 1888, and, - since that time, - led an idle and useless life. His brain seems to have become affected, and he believed that people were trying to poison him. He wrote to Lord Grimthorpe, and others, and also to the Treasury, complaining of Dr Brooks, of Westminster Bridge Rd, whom he threatened to shoot for having supplied him with bad medicines. He is said to have studied medical books by day, and to have rambled about at night, returning frequently with his clothes covered with blood, but little reliance could be placed on the statements made by his mother or his aunt, who both appear to have been of a very excitable disposition. It was found impossible to ascertain his movements on the nights of the Whitechapel murders. The knife found on him was bought in Houndsditch about a week before he was detained in the Infirmary. Cutbush was a nephew of the late Supt. Executive.

Now the Whitechapel Murderer had 5 victims and 5 victims only, - his murders were:

(1) 31st Aug '88. Mary Ann Nichols - at Buck's Row - who was found with her throat cut - & with (slight) stomach mutilation.

(2) 8th Sept '88 Annie Chapman - Hanbury Street: throat cut - stomach & private parts badly mutilated & some of the entrails placed round the neck.

(3) 30th Sept '88. Elizabeth Stride - Berner's Street: throat cut, but nothing in the shape of mutilation attempted, & on same date (4) Catherine Eddowes - Mitre Square, throat cut & very badly mutilation, both of face and stomach.

(5) 9th November. Mary Jane Kelly - Millers Court, throat cut, and the whole of the body mutilated in the most ghastly manner.

The last murder is the only one that took place in a room, and the murderer must have been at least two hours engaged. A photo was taken of the woman, as she was found lying on the bed, without seeing which it is impossible to imagine the awful mutilation.

With regard to the double murder which took place on 30th Sept. There is no doubt but that the man was disturbed by some Jews who drove up to a Club (close to which the body of Elizabeth Stride was (bound) and that he then, 'mordum satiatus', went in search of a further victim whom he found at Mitre Square.

It will be noticed that the fury of the mutilations increased in each case, and, seemingly, the appetite only became sharpened by indulgence. It seems, then, highly improbable that the murderer would have suddenly stopped in November '88, and been content to recommence operations by merely prodding a girl behind some two years and 4 months afterwards. A much more rational theory is that the murderer's brain gave way altogether after his awful glut in Miller's Court, and that he immediately committed suicide, or, as a possible alternative, was found to be so hopelessly mad by his relations, that he was by them confined to some asylum.

No one ever saw the Whitechapel Murderer, many homicidal maniacs were suspected, but no shadow of proof would be thrown on any one. I may mention the cases of three men, any one of whom would have been more likely than Cutbush to have committed this series of murders:-

(1) A Mr M. J. Druitt, said to be a doctor and of good family, who disappeared at the time of the Miller's Court murder, and whose body (which was said to have been upwards of a month in the water) was found in the Thames on 31st Dec. - or about 7 weeks after that murder. He was sexually insane and from private info I have little doubt but that his own family believed him to have been the murderer.

(2) Kosminski, a Polish Jew and resident in Whitechapel. This man became insane owing to many years indulgence in solitary vices. He had a great hatred of women, especially of the prostitute class, and had strong homicidal tendencies: he was removed to a lunatic asylum about March 1889. There were many crimes connected with this man which made him a strong 'suspect'.

*(3) **Michael Ostrog, a Russian doctor, and a convict, who was subsequently detained in a lunatic asylum as a homicidal maniac. This man's antecedents were of the worst possible type, and his whereabouts at the time of the murders could never be ascertained.***

And now with regard to a few of the inaccuracies and misleading statements made by the 'Sun'. In its issue of 14th Feb., it is stated that the writer had in his possession a facsimile of the knife with which the murders were committed. This knife (which for some unexplained reason has, for the last 3 years, been kept by Insp. Race, instead of being sent to Prisoners' Property Store) was traced and it was found to have been purchased in Houndsditch in Feb.'91 or two years and 3 months after the Whitechapel murders ceased!

The statement, too, that Cutbush 'spent a portion of the day in making rough drawings of the bodies of women, and of their mutilations' is based solely on the fact that two scribble drawings of women in indecent postures were found torn up in Cutbush's room. The head and body of one of these had been cut from some fashion plate, and legs were added to show a woman's naked thighs and pink stockings.

In the issue of 15th Inst, it is said that a light overcoat was among the things found in Cutbush's house, and that a man in a light overcoat was seen talking to a woman in Backchurch Lane whose body with arms attached was found in Pinchin St. This is hopelessly incorrect! On 10th Sept.'89 the naked body, with arms, of a woman was found in some sacking under a railway arch in Pinchin St: the head and legs were never found nor was the woman ever identified. She had been killed at least 24 hours before the remains (which had seemingly been brought from a distance) were discovered. The stomach was slit up by a cut, and the head and legs had been severed in a manner identical with that of the woman whose remains were discovered in the Thames, in Battersea Park, and on the Chelsea Embankment on 4th June of the same year; and these murders had no connection whatever with the Whitechapel horrors. The Rainham mystery in 1887, and the Whitehall mystery (when portions of a woman's body were found under what is now Scotland Yard) in 1888 were of a similar type to the Thames and Pinchin St. crimes.

It is perfectly untrue to say that Cutbush stabbed six girls behind - this is confounding his case with that of Colicutt.

The theory that the Whitechapel murderer was left-handed, or, at any rate 'ambidextrous', had its origin in the remark made by a doctor who examined the corpse of one of the earliest victims; other doctors did not agree with him.

With regard to the four additional murders ascribed by the writer in the 'Sun' to the Whitechapel fiend:-

(1) The body of Martha Tabram, a prostitute was found on a common staircase in George Yard buildings on 7th August 1888; the body had been repeatedly pierced, probably with a bayonet. This woman had, with a fellow prostitute, been in company of two soldiers in the early part of the evening. These men were arrested, but the second prostitute failed, or refused, to identify, and the soldiers were accordingly discharged.

(2) Alice McKenzie was found with her throat cut (or rather stabbed) in Castle Alley on 17th July 1889; no evidence was forthcoming and no arrests were made in connection with this case. The stab in the throat was of the same nature as in the case of the murder.

(3) Frances Coles in Swallow Gardens, on 13th February 1891- for which Thomas Sadler, a fireman, was arrested, and, after several remands, discharged. It was ascertained at the time that Sadler had sailed for the Baltic on 19th July '89 and was in Whitechapel on the night of 17th idem. He was a man of ungovernable temper and entirely addicted to drink and the company of the lowest prostitutes.

(4) The case of the unidentified woman whose trunk was found in Pinchin St on 10th Sept. 1889 - which had already been dealt with.

M. L. Macnaghten

❝ The last murder is the only one that took place in a room, and the murderer must have been at least two hours engaged ❞

Macnaghten was mistaken on a number of points; Druitt for example was never a doctor; Ostrog was a Polish Jew who was more of a confidence trickster than a killer; while Cutbush was much more violent. Yet these notes of his have served as the basis for most of the serious research undertaken by Ripperologists.

The police were never looking for a serial sexual murderer, they were hunting for their imaginary homicidal lunatic. Druitt alone, of the selected three had never been an asylum inmate; but his suicide brought him into the insane category and this matched police expectations. And all other candidates had to measure up to these same archaic standards.

In Druitt's case, some thirty years of searching by numerous writers has failed to connect him in any way with the murders, or even with Whitechapel, but he went insane at the crucial time and that was enough to list his name as a possible. 'Many homicidal maniacs were suspected...' wrote Macnaghten, and this needs to be stressed over and over again. The police were so convinced that this was what they were looking for that their minds remained closed to the real nature of the killer.

Interestingly enough, only one of the top men at the time of the murders ever rejected Macnaghten's list of madmen. This was Inspector Abberline, the man on the streets in 1888, for in 1903 he named a man who had never even been considered before. His choice was the Polish wife-poisoner, George Chapman. What governed that odd choice? Some writers have mistakenly echoed Abberline's own words and imagined that the Solicitor-General's opening statement at the Chapman trial linked Chapman with Whitechapel. But the trial record proved that Abberline was at fault. The opening speech does *not* place Chapman in Whitechapel at any time, neither does it even place him in the East End in 1888. Since this speech obviously offered no impetus for fresh thoughts, the answer to the Chapman conundrum must lie elsewhere.

Chapter 11

What Manner of Man?

In the 1880s few people understood anything about the varieties and lures of sexual aberrations. When the police were faced with a serial sexual murderer they could only draw on their inadequate experience and conclude that they were being challenged by a madman. Their conclusions would be inevitably coloured by the shallow thinking and prejudices of the day, so even their hypothetical madman was most likely a foreigner and probably not a Christian. It is no accident that the three men listed by Macnaghten are thought of as insane; that two of them are Polish Jews; and that the odd man out is most likely a homosexual.

Our present-day state of knowledge tells us that such a view was far too simplistic and even dangerously wrong. This does not mean that the police of the day were incompetent, they were simply without the experience that alone could give them guidance. Today we have the misfortune to have far too much experience of serial sexual murderers, but that unwanted experience does at least give us knowledge. The systematic study of such killers has shown us what we should look for. Forget the madmen and the obvious types, the killer will not be among them. He will be someone normal-looking, intelligent even, perhaps a pleasant person. Someone like an innocuous next-door neighbour, a man hard to suspect, if at all. These people give no outward signs of the rages within; their secret lives stay submerged; only their victims ever get to glimpse the hidden monster who craves power over them. Such killers are so very different from the old-fashioned stereotypes that once dominated popular - and even police - thinking. They plan, they stalk, they savour every stage of the hunt, and they are not creatures of impulse. And when their victims are despatched, they then savour the hue and cry, and the fear they engender in the world around them. Looking back at everything that was written about the Whitechapel murders, only one man (a reporter) was able to come anywhere near to an accurate assessment of the killer's personality. His views, as published in the *New York Herald* ((London ed.) on 21 July 1889) are remarkable for their foresight:

Second to our anonymous newsman comes Dr Thomas Bond. In his report on the five victims he says:

The murderer must have been a man of physical strength and of great coolness and daring. There is no evidence that he had an accomplice. He must in my opinion be a man subject to periodical attacks of Homicidal and erotic mania. The character of the mutilations indicate that the man may be in a condition sexually, that may be called satyriasis. It is of course possible that the Homicidal impulse may have developed from a revengeful or brooding condition of

21 July 1889 **NEW YORK HERALD** London Ed.

I. have been trying for a year to form in my mind a harmonious conception of the murderer, and had been unable to do so. I have had some experience with various forms of mania in several lunatic asylums as an amateur specialist, but the combination of qualities which the Whitechapel murderer presents is so incongruous, that I could not reconcile them in one man. To me - and I have watched the case closely, been on the ground shortly after every murder, and seen every victim - the man is a sane man with a blood mania, who is well educated, excessively keen, excessively cool, and more determined and resolute than ninety-nine men in a hundred. He is also a humorist in his ghastly way. He combines with his horrible purpose a mockery of the police which savours of fun...

the mind, or that Religious Mania may have been the original disease, but I do not think either hypothesis is likely. The murderer in external appearance is quite likely to be a quiet inoffensive looking man probably middle-aged and neatly and respectably dressed. I think he must be in the habit of wearing a cloak or overcoat or he could hardly have escaped notice in the streets if the blood on his hands or clothes were visible.

Assuming the murderer to be such a person as I have just described he would probably be solitary and eccentric in his habits, also he is most likely to be a man without regular occupation, but with some small income or pension. He is possibly living among respectable persons who have some knowledge of his character and habits and who may have grounds for suspicion that he is not quite right in his mind at times. Such persons would probably be unwilling to communicate suspicions to the Police for fear of trouble or notoriety, whereas if there were a prospect of reward it might overcome their scruples.

The dominant view of the day, however, still directed the search towards the madmen. 'Enquiries were also made,' says a police report of 19 October 1888 'to trace three insane medical students who had attended London Hospital Result two traced, one gone abroad.' Earlier, on 11 September, Doctors Cowan and Crabb, informed the police that Joseph Issenschmidt, who had spent ten weeks in the Colney Hatch Asylum, was most likely the Ripper. Issenschmidt was once more taken to an asylum on 17 September 1888, and while locked up there the murders continued, so his innocence was established beyond doubt. And there were other mentally disturbed men around in the area who were taken in for questioning or harassed by ignorant mobs. The fallacies of the day continued to rule.

From his chosen bolt-hole the real killer could afford to gloat and smile. He was certain that no trace of wildness or madness would ever govern his features, his speech or his movements. All his actions were calculated, controlled, and designed to promote in others a feeling of trust and ease. His civilized veneer warded off all suspicions. His peaks only came at the time of killing. Even so, with time, this man proved to be vulnerable.

So who was he? In 1930 Fleet Street journalist Bernard O'Donnell began to ask that question. It did not come to him spontaneously, but was put in his mind by Hayter Preston, editor of the *Sunday Referee*. Preston was a friend of the poet Victor Neuburg, and Neuburg had once been one of Alaister Crowley's dupes. His health had been threatened by Crowley's demands until Crowley's business manager took pity on him and helped him break away. This business manager was an American lady called Vittoria Cremers.

She was the widow of Baron Louis Cremers, at one time attached to the diplomatic corps at the Russian Embassy in Washington. She also had a strange story to tell about the Whitechapel murders.

Neuburg had heard of some of the events from her own lips, but not enough to be able to give O'Donnell material for a story, so Preston urged O'Donnell to visit the lady at her retreat, somewhere in Caerleon-on-Usk, in Monmouthshire. O'Donnell was intrigued. He was certain that no one had ever claimed to have known the Ripper intimately. So this had to be very different from the usual Fleet Street assignment. O'Donnell was inspired enough to make the long trip to Caerleon. But his journey was wasted; the lady had returned to London, without leaving a forwarding address. O'Donnell was too good a journalist to despair. The capital was an enormous place but someone must know her whereabouts. And he

was right. His searches paid off and he tracked the lady down to 34 Marius Road in Balham, South West London.

On his first visit he found her a formidable person, but she soon came to appreciate his professional zeal, and so, in 1930 Vittoria Cremers began to unburden herself at length for the first time. She wrote small pieces for him over four years until at last O'Donnell was able to view her complete memoirs for the years 1888 to 1891. She gave him all her reminiscences without taking anything for them. She was completely without mercenary motives.

But the one thing about this lady that impressed O'Donnell more than anything else was her ability to talk to him about events that must have been alarming, in a quiet, matter-of-fact manner; and without any attempt to colour her accounts. This, he came to realize, resulted from her basic view of life; she was almost fatalistic in her beliefs. From his angle this was all to the good. The story he wanted would be sensational enough without any added colourings or exaggerations prompted by remembered fears or hates.

O'Donnell himself was never to publish her story. He spent some years trying to trace the main character in her pages, but was thwarted. The man she wrote and talked about did not exist in public records. There were articles of his, even a book; but no birth certificate, no marriage-lines, and no trace of his death.

There was a good reason for this. The name he was known by was assumed; and his true identity was not established during O'Donnell's lifetime. But, the Cremers memoirs in the end proved to be one of the most significant documents in the whole history of the hunt for Jack the Ripper.

For the first time, we have believable and verifiable testimony from someone who was close to the killer day after day for over eighteen months. When she wrote, she recorded facts that she could not have drawn from the literature of the day. Some of these facts were only checkable as late as the 1960s. All the documentation and testimony we can now draw on confirms her story as reliable, accurate and invaluable; and she was not alone in naming her colleague as the Ripper. Others who knew him well, thought the same.

Her story began in New York in 1886, when in a bookshop, she came across a copy of *Light on the Path* by Mabel Collins. It was one of the treasured books of the Theosophical movement and its opening words read: 'These rules are written for all disciples, attend you to them.' For some reason the words struck

deep into Cremers and she felt impelled to buy the book, 'It was as though some unseen force was driving me to take it home with me to read,' she explained.

This one, slim book was to change her life. First, it made such a profound impression on her that she eagerly joined the American Theosophical Society. Then, in 1888 on arriving in Britain she went to the HQ of the British Society to enrol and there met Madame Helena Petrova Blavatsky, the greatest name in Theosophy. Blavatsky, on learning that Cremers had been involved in publishing, asked her to take over the business side of the society's monthly magazine Lucifer, and Cremers agreed.

Work at the Theosophists' headquarters in Holland Park (17 Lansdowne Road) was unexacting and Cremers often dreamed of meeting up with the woman who had inspired her. She now knew that Mabel Collins was a notable novelist and a one-time spiritualist medium. She also learned that Mabel lived near at hand, so a meeting was just a matter of time.

But the full story of that meeting and its fateful consequences must be left to Vittoria Cremers herself. What follows are her own words. The only changes made involve the supplying of full names where she used initials.

Chapter 12

The Fateful Paths Converge

The events of 1888 were crystal clear in Vittoria Cremers' mind when she unfolded her story in the 1930s. In her detached, unemotional fashion she recalled her first meeting with the alluring Mabel Collins, and her brief contact with the turmoil surrounding the Ripper murders.

It was inevitable that I should meet Mabel Collins at some time or other, because she was associate editress of Lucifer and our paths were bound to cross. I had settled down to my job at No. 17 and like the rest of those engaged in Theosophical work, lived there with Madame Blavatsky. Among others prominent in the Theosophical movement here, were Dr Archibald Keightley and his cousin Bertram.

But it was Mabel Collins in whom I was chiefly interested, and when one day, she strolled into the Lucifer office in company with the Keightleys and began to chat with me in a most friendly way I felt strongly drawn towards her. She was living at 34 Clarendon Road, the garden of which backed onto that of 17 Lansdowne Road. So that Helena Blavatsky and Mabel Collins were in the habit of signalling to each other across the gardens whenever they wanted to see one another. In addition to her theosophical work and the novels she wrote, Mabel Collins was also the fashion writer on Edmund Yates' periodical, The World, and I can recall her dashing about London in hansom cabs in pursuit of news on the latest fashions.

I told her that Light on the Path had been the direct cause of my joining the Theosophical movement, and as a result

THE FATEFUL PATHS CONVERGE

I was invited to her home, and from that time onwards we became close friends.

One day in the December of 1888, I went into the big room behind my office. It was the sanctum where the Blavatsky Lodge was held, and the moment I entered I sensed a state of suppressed excitement in the room. There stood the two Keightleys, one on either side of Helena Blavatsky who was seated at a card table with a newspaper spread out before her. The two men were leaning over her shoulder plying her with questions the gist of which I gathered in snatches such as, 'Jack the Ripper - Yes - Is it true? - Yes - Did Crawford write it? - Yes – Black Magic'.

I was young in years - about twenty-eight - and densely, pathetically ignorant of things occult. The words I heard meant absolutely nothing to me. I was still but a newcomer to the Theosophical movement, and so far as the Ripper murders were concerned knew little beyond the shrieking headlines. Such things did not interest me and I did not read the reports. As for Black Magic, I had never heard of such a thing anymore than I knew that the Earl of Crawford and Balcarres was one of the leading occultists of that day.

I only know that when I went into the big room on that December afternoon, the occupants were in a state of tension. Later on when I chanced to mention it to Mabel Collins she explained that the article over which they were poring was one written by Lord Crawford for Pall Mall Gazette, suggesting that Jack the Ripper was a Black Magician.

The incident of the article in the Pall Mall Gazette passed from my mind, and I devoted myself to my theosophical studies, seeking from Mabel Collins such enlightenment as I felt she could give on Light on the Path. Somehow I found her either incapable or unwilling to give me any help, but even so I managed to qualify for entry into the Esoteric Section (Secret Section) of the Society of which I was now a fully fledged member.

In 1889 I had occasion to sail for America in connection with certain business, and it was February 1890 before I returned to England breaking my journey to spend a few weeks in Paris. While there I wrote to Mabel Collins inviting her over to stay with me, pointing "in that she could combine business with pleasure as there were several big fashion shows in progress. I received no reply to my letter, and decided that I would look her up when I got to England.

Cremers finally landed in England in early March, after suffering a wretched, all-night Channel-crossing. She made straight for her usual lodging place, run by Mrs Heilmann at 21 Montague Street, off London's Russell Square; there she tumbled straight into bed. Although worn out and tired, she was unable to asleep, her thoughts were in turmoil over Mabel Collins. Was Mabel angry with her, or was she ill? Cremers was so pre-occupied that she actually rose, dressed and went to Mabel's new address in elegant York Terrace, just behind Madame Tussaud's in Marylebone Road.

When she arrived, the maid told her that Mabel Collins was away in Southsea, writing a new novel; the maid gave her the address there, and the very next day Cremers took a train to visit Mabel.

On arriving at the address Cremers was appalled. The contrast between the splendour of York Terrace and this shabby, dingy street was overwhelming. Could it be that Mabel was seeking colour for her new novel? Or did this mean she had something to hide?

At the drab uninviting house, an unkempt, slatternly looking woman answered the door and led her along a narrow, dingy passage to a flight of stairs. The stairs led to a poorly furnished bedroom on the first floor. As Cremers relates:

It was a comfortless-looking place containing an unmade single bed, a dressing-table with a few cheap china ornaments upon it; and, with the cinders of a previous fire still in the grate, it presented an utterly cheerless appearance.

I began to pace up and down to keep myself warm. I wished I had not come. Then I heard the front door open, the murmur of voices, one unmistakably Mabel Collins', the other a man's. Then came the quiet shutting of the door followed by footsteps hurriedly coming up the stairs. A moment later Mabel Collins burst into the room in a flurry of embarrassment; or so it seemed to me.

'Well, Vittoria - so you've caught me at last... How are you?'

That was her first greeting. We neither kissed nor shook hands for people in the occult movement dispense with all conventions of that kind. Personality is avoided as much as possible, although one must be natural and one's acts not enforced.

Mabel Collins flung herself onto the unmade bed and settled herself Eastern fashion. It was over a year since I had seen her and there was much on both sides to talk about. But Mabel Collins rattled on about nothing in particular until suddenly she paused and regarded me closely.

'Do you remember an article in the Pall Mall Gazette about Rider Haggard's She? she asked. It was signed "D'O", if you remember?'

I said that I remembered her mentioning the article to me early in 1889, but I had never read it, and could not recall the signature of the writer.

Do you remember that I told you I had written to the author care of the Gazette? she then asked.

'No, I can't say that I do,' was my reply.

'Well - I did write to him, and after some weeks received a reply. It was only a few lines saying that the writer was ill in hospital, but as soon as he was better he would write and make an appointment. Again some weeks passed by before I heard anything and then a letter arrived from a Dr D'Onston making an appointment - a marvellous man, Vittoria, a great magician who had wonderful magical secrets.'

She paused to light another cigarette, for she was smoking furiously throughout our talk. Then she went on:

'He's here with me now - still very ill. I'm taking care of him - as soon as he is better we are coming back to London, and we will all go into business together. The three of us.'

I made no comment.

She rose from the bed, and smiling, said: 'But it's cold up here; let's go downstairs where it is warm, and we'll have tea. You will be able to meet D'Onston, for he will soon be back having just gone out for a short walk.'

It required no powers of deduction on my part to realize that D'Onston had been sent out while Mabel Collins told me of her association with him. Anyway the suggestion of tea was very welcome, and I gladly followed her down the stairs. A fire and tea went right home, but her mention of a 'marvellous man' and a 'great magician' meant nothing to me.

Having thawed out over tea, my tongue became loosened and I rattled on about my Paris trip, the nature of my business there, and my meeting with Sarah Bernhardt. I did full justice to the meal provided, and we were about halfway through tea when there was the sound of a key grating in the lock of the front door.

'Here he is...' exclaimed Mabel Collins.

I rose and pushed my chair nearer the wall to make room for the 'marvellous man' whom I assumed would be glad of a hot cup of tea.

'Oh - you needn't bother, Vittoria,' commented Mabel Collins in a casual voice, 'he never eats.'

This statement struck me as very peculiar, but I was to recall it later on when I knew more about Dr D'Onston. I had no time to make any reply however, for by this time he had entered the room so quietly that I was surprised to find him there. I noticed afterwards that there was an uncanny absence of sound in all his movements, and I can honestly say, that throughout the years of our association he was the most soundless human creature I ever knew.

I found myself looking up into the face of a tall fair haired man of unassuming appearance. A man at whom one would not look twice. He held a cap in one hand while under his arm was tucked - in true military fashion - a short cane. I was not unduly impressed. To me there was nothing of the 'marvellous man' about him, and yet - there was an indefinable something.

'So this is Vittoria?' he remarked as he took my hand.

I nodded assent and Mabel broke in.

'I have told her all about you,' she said, 'so there is no need for an introduction.'

Dr D'Onston moved noiselessly over to an armchair in which he seated himself. I had noticed that his voice was pleasant and cultured...

As for myself I was busily sizing up the man sitting opposite me...it was a habit of mine. The sum total of my estimate of D'Onston was nil - absolutely nil - gentle, silent - one who would remain calm in any crisis - maybe because he was ill. I wondered what the matter with him was?

That was the chaotic burden of my summing-up of him between snatches of conversation. I also indulged in a mental analysis of his physical qualities.

Tall — not an ounce of superfluous flesh upon him — military bearing unmistakable and a suggestion of strength and power. Pale; his face had a queer pallor - not a particle of colour anywhere; underlip, pink - upper lip hidden by a fair moustache. Fair hair, thinning at the sides - teeth slightly discoloured (from pipe-smoking I decided).

But it was his eyes which impressed me most. They were pale blue, and - there was not a vestige of life or sparkle in them. They were eyes which one might expect to find set in the face of a patient in the anaemic ward of any hospital.

One other thing impressed me about D'Onston. That was his appearance of super-cleanliness. He looked as though he had just emerged from the bathroom; he was well-groomed about the head, and his clothes, though obviously old and worn, appeared to have suffered from assiduous brushing rather than wear and tear.

Such was my first meeting with Dr Roslyn D'Onston as he called himself...

Cremers' short visit to Southsea convinced her that it was more than the sharing of occult interests that tied Mabel and D'Onston together. She saw that Mabel was deeply infatuated with this enigmatic man, and she was right. The man may have seemed to be a nobody, but perhaps there were hidden depths, and again she was right.

A fortnight later, when Mabel and D'Onston returned to London, Mabel had a problem: where was D'Onston going to stay? She was so prominent as a novelist, Theosophist and socialite that she had to be discreet, and protect her reputation. Cremers, at once, came to her rescue and persuaded Mrs Heilmann to house D'Onston for a while. It turned out to be a short while indeed, as Cremers explains:

He only stayed for a few weeks because he appeared never to eat anything, and like a good landlady, Mrs Heilmann became very worried.

As she put it to me: 'Those who don't eat die, and I don't want him to die on my hands'...I learned later that during one of his many wanderings over the earth, he had been wounded in the stomach, and that a Chinese slug was still lodged in his intestines, this being the cause of his illness and lack of appetite. Mrs Heilmann asked me to persuade him to find other accommodation, but fortunately the difficulty straightened itself out.

Mabel Collins had followed up the suggestion she mooted to me at Southsea about going into business together, and we all three engaged in discussing the project. D'Onston, said Mabel Collins, was possessed of certain little-known recipes for beauty creams and potions, which she thought could be turned to advantage. Beauty parlours as we know them today, were practically non-existent in the nineties, but feminine vanity was by no means lacking, and I felt that the idea might prove a good business proposition.

Mabel Collins and I put up the money, and D'Onston provided the recipes from which the various unguents and lotions were prepared. We formed a company named the Pompadour Cosmetique Company, and took premises in Baker Street on the site where Baker Street Tube Station now stands. It was then a street of houses and our office must have been just opposite the fictional residence of Sherlock Holmes.

We had an office on the first floor, consisting of one large room, where all the business was conducted and the treatments' made up, and a smaller room immediately behind it. The second floor was occupied by a private family while I had a flat on the third floor. The problem of D'Onston's accommodation was solved by letting him live in the small back room on the first floor.

This was a suggestion of Mabel Collins' and it certainly was a way out of our difficulty. It was she who furnished it for him in a kind of monastic comfort. There was just a bed and table, a wash-stand (no toilet basins with H & C in those days), a chair and a huge zinc bath. I had my own maid; part of her duties was to prepare D'Onston's morning bath, and I can assure you that in the matter of his daily ablutions, he was fastidious to the point of fanaticism.

Cremers' new business interests did not interfere with her work for the magazine *Lucifer*. Since she knew D'Onston was always hard-up, she persuaded Blavatsky to commission an article from him. His piece of November 1890, was called *African Magic* and it contained some chilling revelations. But at the time, Cremers' had no idea of its importance. In fact, as she testifies:

I did not see the article and never bothered to read it till it was brought to my notice years later in 1931. Even if I had read it at the time, I doubt whether I should fully have understood it, and I certainly would not have associated the writer with the Ripper crimes which, by the end of 1890 had almost faded from public memory.

Chapter 13

The Mask Begins to Slip

Initially then, Cremers summed up D'Onston, as inoffensive. She was so dismissive of the man that she blinded herself to the fact that he could be anything other than innocuous. The notion that he could be cold, hard, brutal killer; someone to dread and fear, never once crossed her mind. At first, in her open, trusting way she treated him as a friend, and provided him with a good listener one who didn't probe, moralize or judge. But her view of him began to change dramatically when she lived and worked alongside at their place in Baker Street. It was then that her easy and compliant attitude led D'Onston to open up to her in a singular way and reveal, bit by bit, his true character. Cremers relates how her doubts about him began to grow:

The first time I ever really got behind the mind of D'Onston occurred one evening when I returned to Baker Street and was mounting the first I light of stairs to enter the office. As I reached the landing I saw D'Onston standing outside the door of his room. What intrigued me however, was that he appeared to be drawing some sort of sign upon it with his thumb.

There he stood, silent as the grave, an expression of the utmost solemnity on his face. As I passed him, I noticed that he was tracing with his thumb the outline of a triangle on the door. It seemed such a childish thing for a grown-up man to do, that I felt amused as well as amazed.

I said nothing but simply passed on into the office. A few seconds elapsed and then the door was silently opened and D'Onston entered the room closing the

> " There he stood, silent as the grave, an expression
> of the utmost solemnity on his face. "

door gently behind him. He fixed his eyes upon me as I busied myself at the desk, and then asked:

'Did you notice what I was doing, Vittoria?'

'Yes, D'Onston,' I replied, smiling at his serious expression. 'You were drawing something or other on the door, weren't you?'

'Did you notice what it was?'

Looked to me like a triangle'.

'It was a triangle.'

'But you'd got it upside down.'

D'Onston smiled coldly. 'Yes, Vittoria,' he said. 'It was "upside down", as you describe it, and I'll tell you why.'

He seated himself upon one corner of the desk, and then went on:

'Years ago a friend of mine dropped in just before nightfall and suggested a walk. I told him I would run upstairs for my pipe and join him in the hall. I dashed up to my room and went across to the mantelpiece for my pipe.

'Then as I turned to go downstairs I suddenly sensed some horrible Presence outside the open door. I stood still, unable to move so petrified was I with terror. I felt that I dared not venture outside that door - that if I did I should drop down dead from sheer fright.

'At last I summoned up sufficient willpower to creep to the door and peer out. There was nothing to be seen, Vittoria. I scurried down the stairs to join my friend as though the whole of Hell was at my heels. Together we went out into the night, I was in a sweat of fear of something, I knew not what. Only once in my life since that day Vittoria, have I known the fear of that Presence. Later on I learned how to guard against its intrusion by making the sign of the triangle on the door of my room before entering. It is a thing I never fail to do.

This was quite true as I discovered during our residence in Baker Street, for on several other occasions I witnessed the same weird performance. More than once I chaffed him about it when I came upon him in the act.

'Keeping the spooks out I would remark, but he never replied and never ceased to complete his 'upside down' triangle. I had

THE MASK BEGINS TO SLIP

not the least idea at the time that there was any Magical significance either Black or White, about this sign of the triangle nor that its inversion indicated the Black Art. D'Onston said nothing about it, and beyond appearing a silly thing to do, his action made no impression upon me.

As for his story of the 'horrible Presence', it faintly recalled the awe inspiring description of the Presence which figured in Bulwer Lytton's Zanoni. I had read this book on the recommendation of Helena Blavatsky soon after I joined her. To those who may not have read this very fine work I would explain that at one period of the story Zanoni endeavours to invoke the friendly spirit Adonai; instead he found at his side 'the Evil Omen, the implacable Foe, with exultation and malice burning from its hell-lit eyes. . . As an iceberg, the breath of that Presence froze the air; as a cloud it filled the chamber and blackened the stars front heaven.'

And then comes the terrible threat from this hideous Thing.

'Thou art returned to the Threshold,' it tells Zanoni. 'Thou, whose steps have trodden the verges of the Infinite! And, as the goblin of its fancy seizes on a child in the dark, mighty one, who would conquer Death, I seize upon thee.'

Fiction! it may be said. Maybe, but those beliefs were a grim reality to Bulwer Lytton, through several of whose works runs the same strain of mysticism; just as was D'Onston's belief in the Presence which had scared him so thoroughly, a reality.

Of course I had no knowledge of D'Onston's association with Bulwer Lytton till forty years later when Bernard O'Donnell brought the Borderland article to my notice. At the time of which I am writing, it was only a casual recollection of Lytton's creature Zanoni which flashed through my mind when D'Onston related his story about The Dweller on the Threshold.

In drawing attention to Lytton's novel, Cremers was very much on the right track. This work was of enormous significance for many caught up in the thralls of magical thinking. Blavatsky borrowed from it in creating her *Isis Unveiled*. It was also drawn on by the creators of magical societies, like clergyman Charles Leadbeater, coroner Wynn Wescott and antiquarian Kenneth Mackenzie. In short it was taken seriously, as a veiled message to an elite. But its teachings about the Presence, were not elitist; they were, and are still, shared by hordes of people within the Christian churches and within other religions.

Whenever an exorcism takes place, the idea is invoked. Listen to the words of Roman Catholic exorcist, Malachi Martin:

From the moment the exorcist enters the room, a peculiar feeling seems to hang in the very air. From that moment in any genuine exorcism and onward through its duration, everyone in the room is aware of some alien Presence. This indubitable sign of possession is as unexplainable and unmistakable as it is inescapable. All the signs of possession, however blatant or grotesque, however subtle or debatable, seem both to pale before and to be marshalled in the face of this Presence.

There is no sure physical trace of this Presence, but everyone feels it. You have to experience it to know it; you cannot locate it spatially – beside or above or without the possessed, or over in the corner of under the bed or hovering in mid air.

In one sense, the Presence is nowhere, and this magnifies the terror... Invisible and intangible, the <u>Presence</u> claws at the humanness of those gathered in the room...

By openly acknowledging his fear of the *Presence*, D'Onston showed the extent of his dependence on magical ideas. But by employing his protective symbol, he revealed his belief that he had power enough to control even the forces of darkness. Such a delusion is enough to make a warped man contemptuous of humane values. Such a man lives for the exercise of power and the total annihilation of anyone bent on thwarting him. In D'Onston's case these drives were well concealed at first; with time he grew bolder, more openly contemptuous and more loose tongued.

Chapter 14

A Glimpse of Brutality

It was in an off-hand way that D'Onston first revealed his indifference to the sanctity of human life. One afternoon he spoke to Cremers about an incident involving his favourite cousin. This cousin was in love with a girl who had rejected him as a suitor but had accepted him as a friend. One day the cousin came to D'Onston in great anguish. The girl he loved had been made pregnant by another man and this seducer had deserted her and left the country.

D'Onston asked for a handkerchief belonging to the girl and said:

'Tell her that neither of you will see nor hear from me until I can send or bring proof that she has been avenged.'

His hunt for the seducer took all of fifteen months and at last he caught up with him in California.

'I dipped the handkerchief in his blood,' said D'Onston, 'and on my return flung it into her lap without a word.'

After summarising this story Cremers continued:

I remember thinking what a braggart he was and yet his story was not told in any sense of vainglory but simply in matter-of-fact tones; tones such as one would use in recalling an ordinary incident of life. That is how it struck me at the time, and I attached no more importance to it than that.

D'Onston's recitals were always spontaneous, seeming to arise out of nothing particular in the way of conversation. It was not in response to any questioning by me that he told his stories, for from earliest days. I have been possessed of an almost abnormal faculty never to ask questions, never to interrupt a conversation, but allow a speaker to carry on with his or her talk to the bitter end. So it was with D'Onston. I never invited a confidence and never broke into anything he might be telling me. In fact, looking back, I think I must have been the most silent of any of his listeners. It had always been my belief that if I was destined to have certain knowledge, it would come to me without my seeking. Consequently when he related his varied and colourful experiences to me, I did not trouble to question his stories, but appeared to accept them. And in repeating them now, I am doing so, not in consecutive order as they may have been told to me over the months, but as they occur to me after a lapse of forty years.

For example, I do not precisely remember when he recounted the following experience during a Californian gold rush, he said:

'My mate and I had been weeks prospecting to set up a claim and eventually settled on one which eventually turned out of little account. Some time later it was rumoured that a Chink had found a nugget larger than any hitherto found in those parts. My mate and I put our heads together for we felt sure the Chink would sell his claim, and we decided that we could handle the matter with greater efficiency than a damned Chinaman. We watched and waited for him to make a move towards town to effect a sale. Sure enough things turned out exactly as we anticipated.

'Late one night he set off and we followed him. For a couple of days we were on his heels - unseen. We knew the trail he must travel, and on the second day we managed to get ahead of him and lay in wait behind a rock. Sure enough about three hours later Mr Chinaman came along, and unfortunately for him, as he passed nearby, my mate's pistol accidentally went off.

No details you will observe; no mention of any sequel to that accidental death of the Chink; no information as to what happened to the claim; nothing but a plain un-

ABOVE Westminster Bridge, London at the time of the killings varnished story of villainy, which, whether true or not throws an illuminating light on the working of D'Onston's mind and his attitude towards the taking of human life. Related as casually as when he referred to his slave-trading activities in the Pall Mall Gazette with a brief - 'That by the way.'

I got another glimpse of this callousness when he was relating an experience he had with the Garibaldean army in 1860. First of all he described the ghastly conditions under which he worked.

'I had got my MD,' he said, 'but was not yet in practice when I learned from a friend of the terrible plight the medical services of Garibaldi were in for want of doctors. I at once crossed to Italy and offered my services. The conditions were terrible, Vittoria. There were scarcely any medical supplies, no anaesthetics, very few bandages, while surgical equipment was almost non-existent. I had to perform many an amputation with anaesthetic, and the poor devils I operated on must have suffered agonies. There was nothing else for it, and it was no good being squeamish. More often than not they fainted and knew nothing about it till it was all over. Scores of those I dealt with never came through at all, but I gained a wonderful experience which it would have taken me twenty years to ac-

quire if I had stayed at home.'

I remembered thinking at the time, 'Flint-hearted devil'. His callous reference to the sufferings of those upon whom he operated without anaesthetic; his casual mention that 'scores never came through but I gained a wonderful experience' irked me. That was all it meant to him and I was angry.

In the same callous, indifferent fashion he went on to mention yet another brutal act of his:

'I had gone to bed after days in action without rest or sleep, when I was suddenly awakened by a subaltern who said that a wounded prisoner had just been brought in. The youngster wanted to know what he should do with him. I was only half awake and thoroughly irritable. "Take him outside and shoot him, but leave me in peace!" I told the subaltern, and turned over and went to sleep. My order was carried out to the letter Vittoria, and I may say there was a devil of a row about it; but - what did it matter? The man was an enemy, and that's what enemies are for - to kill.'

After considering these tales Mrs Cremers concluded: 'So much for the outlook of D'Onston, so far as human life was concerned - a matter of small consequence.'

Chapter 15

The Ghost from the Past

In all these reminiscences D'Onston seemed to be unmoved by tenderness, compassion or human warmth, but gradually he began to reveal that he had once been emotionally vulnerable and wounded. An incident from his youth had crippled his capacity to love, as Vittoria Cremers reveals.

All this time I would mention, the association between Mabel Collins and D'Onston, was of the closest nature. I had no doubt in my mind that she was greatly infatuated with him, for in those early days, she could talk of little else, and D'Onston was a regular visitor to her flat behind Madame Tussaud's about two minutes walk from our office.

For myself, I neither liked nor disliked him. He was Mabel Collins' friend and simply part of the day's work so far as the business was concerned. I could not, however, help but notice D'Onston's reactions to the obvious affection shown him by Mabel Collins. She had taken him away to Southsea to recuperate after his illness; she had provided him with his creature needs and comforts; had furnished for him the room in Baker Street; had supplied him with money, and was ready to do anything for his happiness.

As regards D'Onston, I never saw the least sign of any emotional response to this kindness throughout the whole of their association. He was always courteous and polite; but never once did

I notice his eyes light up, or his actions reveal any degree of pleasure when he and Mabel greeted one another.

It was to Mabel Collins that D'Onston confided the story of his shattered romance with a woman named Ada. In due course she unburdened herself of the story to me. And - there was something pathetic about Mabel as she did so. It became clear to me that she had been compelled to realize that whatever the bond existing between her and D'Onston, it only occupied a secondary place in his mind. More than once she made this apparent when discussing her lover.

'D'Onston loved Ada,' she would say. 'Loved her in a way that sometimes frightens me, Vittoria.'

'I didn't think he ever loved anybody but himself,' I told her bluntly; but over and over again when we were talking, she would sadly remark, 'He loved Ada and will never get over her loss. No other woman will ever take her place.'

Now Mabel Collins was an extremely level-headed woman. She had already written a number of books and novels and was extremely popular with those who knew her. And, although I lived in the same house with D'Onston, and was in regular daily contact with him, there can be no doubt that Mabel Collins knew him better than any other living person.

She, more than anyone else, was able to get behind the mind of the quiet, reticent, soundless man who was Roslyn D'Onston. She was a psychologist who had gained a vast knowledge of the human mind, as any reader of Light on the Path will agree.

Consequently, I was more than usually interested when she began to unfold what she referred to as 'the love story' of D'Onston; and when she constantly reiterated, 'He loved Ada,' I quite understood that she did not mean he was sexually attracted to her. Love, not sexual attraction invariably means sacrifice, and Love is sacrifice. And that is what Mabel Collins wanted to convey - D'Onston's readiness to make a sacrifice for Ada.

According to D'Onston, he had at one time held a commission in the Army. Of yeoman family, his father was fairly well off. When the daughter of a wealthy neighbouring family fell in love with D'Onston, the match was looked upon with great favour.

But things were 'not to run well for D'Onston', as Mabel Collins put it. On one of his jaunts to town with some brother officers, he fell in with a woman of the streets to whom he became strongly attracted. On each subsequent visit he made a point of meeting this woman until he found himself wildly in love with her. This was the woman Ada.

I realize now - at this late hour - how my faculty for not asking questions, has resulted in obscurity on many points which, had I been more inquisitive, might have been cleared up. For example, we do not know Ada's surname, or anything else about her. And certainly it never occurred to me that Ada's surname would ever be of any importance, especially at this length of time when it would have been interesting to check up on her existence.

Mabel went on to tell me that D'Onston became so infatuated with Ada that he determined to marry her and take her away from her miserable life. He told his family of his intention and they were aghast. His brother officers were equally shocked, and tried to talk him out of his decision. They reasoned, expostulated, and pointed out the inevitable consequence which would follow any such alliance, but D'Onston was adamant.

Neither the efforts of his officer friends, nor the broken-hearted appeals of his parents had the least effect. He loved Ada and intended to save her from herself.

As for Ada, there appears to have existed - in spite of her mode of life - a certain decency of character. As Mabel told me, 'Ada loved D'Onston, just as he loved her. I am convinced of it, Vittoria.

D'Onston set Ada up in rooms where he used to visit her. To bring him to heel, as it were, his father cut off his allowance with the result that the son's need for money became desperate. Always a gambler, D'Onston was found at the tables more often, plunging more wildly than ever. His misalliance with Ada had been kept a close secret in the family as it was still hoped that D'Onston would get over his infatuation and break with his mistress.

Then, one night he lost a large sum of money. He realised that he could not pay his gambling debts. In desperation he sought out his father and explained his position. What took place at that interview Mabel Collins never learned. There was some sort of scene, and in the end, D'Onston told Mabel, he agreed to give up Ada and marry the heiress.

That same night he journeyed to London. He visited Ada and told her all that had happened; told her that he had come to see her for the last time, but - she would be provided for through his father's solicitor.

There were no tears, no recriminations, no protests. 'Ada loved me,' D'Onston told Mabel Collins. But, before they said goodbye they entered into a solemn pledge, that dead or alive they would meet at midnight on the anniversary of their parting, and their meeting place should be the middle of Westminster Bridge where they had first met.

So they parted, and within an hour of her lover's departure Ada threw a shawl over her head and walked to the spot where they had met a few months before, determined that she would not stand in the way of her lover's career, Ada flung herself into the river below.

According to what D'Onston told Mabel Collins the story of his association with Ada came out at the inquest but already he was beyond all care; for, as a result of the anguish which gripped him when he heard of her tragic death, he went down with brain fever, and subsequently had to go aboard to recuperate.

About a fortnight prior to the anniversary of Ada's death, D'Onston returned to England, still broken in health that he could scarcely walk and had to be wheeled about in a bath-chair. He had resigned his commission in the Army; his prospective marriage to the heiress had also come to an end. This did not matter to D'Onston, whose one thought now was to keep the appointment which he had made with Ada on the night she took her life; that 'living or dead' they would meet on Westminster Bridge on the anniversary of their parting. On that night, D'Onson ordered his man to wheel him to the bridge and on reaching the Westminster end, he made him stop. D'Onston got out, and telling the man to remain where he was, he tottered along to the middle of the bridge. He leaned over the parapet from which Ada had hurled herself to death twelve months before; Big Ben chimed the midnight hour, and then (D'Onston told Mabel) he head the click-lack of heels coming towards him. The sound came nearer and nearer and paused beside him. He strained his eyes but could see nothing. Minutes passed by. There was no further sound of any kind, and so, with lagging feet he returned to the end of the bridge where his man awaited him.

'Did you see anyone pass this way?' D'Onston asked.

'No sir', replied the servant. 'I saw nothing, but I distinctly heard the sound of footsteps, but although I looked saw nobody.'

D'Onston entered his chair and was wheeled home.

When Mabel Collins told me this story, I remarked, 'Fiction! He was imagining things.' At that time you must remember, I had no knowledge of the contents of the Pall Mall Gazette or Lucifer articles and those in Borderland (which I also knew nothing about till years later) had not been written.

It was not until sometime later that the story of Ada assumed any degree of significance in my mind, and then only after my suspicions had been aroused that D'Onston was in fact Jack the Ripper. That however, comes later in my story.

BELOW
Mabel
Collins

> " Ada loved me, D'Onston told Mabel Collins. But, before they said goodbye they entered into a solemn pledge, that dead or alive they would meet at midnight on the anniversary of their parting "

It is ironic that Cremers knew that the take of the lost love though true in substance, was drastically altered in parts. But even if she had realized this she would still have failed to discover just how this talk embodied one of the trigger-factors that led to the Whitechapel murders. Neither would she have known that the full story could lead to the truth about D'Onston's past and to the identity of his 'vanished' wife. And yet this full story had actually appeared in print not once, but three times over!

Chapter 16

Sordid Symbols

Without the real keys to D'Onston's history, Cremers had to rely on the guarded references D'Onston made from time to time. As she recollects:

Apart from the self-revelations contained in the stories he told me, D'Onston displayed a strange reticence regarding himself. Except when describing his magical experiences or his adventures abroad, he seldom talked of his own being. Regarding his private life, his origin, or his family, never a word.

On several occasions Mabel Collins endeavoured to break through this reserve but without success..

'Who the devil are you?' she once asked him point-blank.

But D'Onston simply smiled his usual lifeless smile, 'Does it matter?' he replied and uttered not another word.

I remember too my curiosity when he brought to me the article for Lucifer. I just glanced at the title and then noticed that it was 'by Tautriadelta'.

'Why D'Onston...' I commented, 'what a funny way of signing yourself. Why don't you sign your name?'

He only smiled the slow inscrutable smile in which there was never a trace of mirth.

'That is my own name,' he answered.

'Tautriadelta?' I repeated. 'But what does it all mean? It seems so strange to me.'

'Yes Vittoria,' said D'Onston. 'A strange signature indeed, but one that means a devil of a lot if you only knew. A devil of a lot!' he repeated with sardonic emphasis.

'But what does it stand for?' I enquired, breaking through my usual rule never to ask questions.

LEFT Dr Edward Getsinger gave an insight into the mentality of D'Onston.

'Before the Captivity,' D'Onston explained, 'the Hebrew was always shown in the form of a Cross. It was the last letter of the sacred alphabet. Tria is the Greek for three, while Delta is the Greek letter D which is written in the form of a triangle. So the completed word signifies Cross-Three-Triangles.

He paused for a moment or two as though reflecting.

'And Vittoria,' he went on, 'there are lots of people who would be interested to know why I use that signature. In fact, the knowledge would create quite a sensation.' And then, as though in defiance, 'But they never will find out, Vittoria, never.'

I did not press the matter because quite frankly it sounded like so much gibberish, and was far above my head. Mabel Collins had told me that he was a most learned man who had a vast knowledge of the Kabbalah, and I accepted her estimate. But - I still could not understand why he had adopted such a strange and involved nom de plume, or why he did not prefer the use of his own name.

That Tautriadelta embodied a taunting reference to murder and mutilation quite eluded Baroness Cremers. But then, it was meant to tantalize. Its hidden meanings were part of the dangerous game of unveiling cherished secrets; but only to those able to understand the rules of the game; only those could pierce the thick veils of deception.

This was in line with the age-old traditions of the occultists, who would sometimes bury three or more meanings in their writings and grow conceited about their abilities to create enigmas and puzzles, and to fool the rest of the world. Dr Edward Getsinger has given us valuable insight into this mentality:

Those among the ancients who were in possession of the ancient mysteries of life and certain secret astronomical cycles never trusted this knowledge to ordinary writing, but devised secret codes by which they conceal their wisdom from the unworthy... As ages progressed other systems were invented until human ingenuity was taxed to the utmost in an endeavour to conceal and yet perpetuate sacred knowledge...

In all my twenty years of experience as a reader of archaic writings I have never encountered such ingenious codes and methods of concealment as are found in the manuscript called Le Tres Sainte Trinosophie.

In only a few instances are complete phrases written in the same alphabet; usually two or three forms of writing are employed, with letters written upside down, reversed, or with the text written backwards...

Is it any wonder that Cremers never attempted to decipher D'Onston's strange name? Much more puzzling at the time was Cremers' discovery of some unwholesome foul pieces of candle found burning on D'Onston's mantelpiece.

Good God, D'Onston,' I exclaimed. 'Where on earth did you get those filthy-looking candles?'

'I made them,' he answered quietly.

'Made them?' I queried in surprise, and then after taking another look at them, I should think you did, I have never seen such grubby- looking things in all my life. But what are they made of?'

D'Onston made no answer to the last question, but simply remarked. 'It is an experiment.'

'What - going into the candle business now?' I retorted jokingly, but he only answered with a surly 'No'.

But two years earlier, in an article on the Whitechapel murders D'Onston had scorned all evasion and revealed that candles 'made from human fat' were essential for the practice of Black Magic. Equally essential, he had revealed, was 'a preparation made from a certain portion of the body of a harlot'.

Chapter 17

A Scarlet Woman?

Harlots, murders and grotesque rituals were far from Vittoria Cremers' mind at this time. She was much more concerned with Mabel Collins' sexual reputation which became besmirched in a bitter war of words raging in the Theosophical Society. Blavatsky was now being challenged for leadership by Colonel Olcott and A. P. Sinett and, although Cremers stood aloof from all this, she was drawn in when Mabel Collins sided with Sinett.

The struggle was fought with cruel, harsh words; malicious charges were thrown recklessly around; and Mabel's character was blackened. It was now alleged that her novel *The Blossom and the Fruit* had once contained an ending endorsing Black Magic of the darkest dye. Blavatsky, herself, had intervened before its publication and had rewritten the final chapters to make it pure in doctrine. Other 'revelations' charged that Mabel was addicted to sexual perversions! Cremers only came to know smears after Blavatsky decided to purge her staff of all who were disloyal to her. Cremers relates:

One day Helena Blavatsky sent for me. 'My dear,' she began, 'I must ask you to give up your association with Mabel Collins.'

I told her that i would do nothing of the kind, whereupon she that she had been compelled to ask Mabel Collins to leave the Society because of her conduct with the Keightleys. She told me that Mabel

> **" Harlots, murders and grotesque rituals were far from Vittoria Cremers' mind at this time "**

Collins was at one time engaged to Dr Archibald Keightley, and that they had taken part in Tantric Worship performing Black Magic Rites, as a result of which they had got into serious trouble. 'I had the greatest difficulty in extricating them from the mess into which they got themselves,' Helena Blavatsky told me.

I promptly told her that I would on no account give up my friendship with Mabel Collins until I myself found her an unfit associate.

Helena Blavatsky shrugged her shoulders. 'Then I am afraid I must ask you also to leave the Society.'

'I shall certainly do so,' I answered, though not without regret, for I was a staunch believer in the faith; but I was furious. At once I sought out Mabel Collins, who, the moment she saw me laughed aloud.

'The old lady's been after you,' she said; and then, 'I knew you'd get it.'

In anger I told her of the accusations Helena Blavatsky had made in giving reasons why I should break with her (Mabel Collins).

It was then the latter's turn to fly into a rage. She began to threaten an action for defamation of character; but things did not go as far as that, although scandal ensued with the result that many of the best people dropped out of the movement.

Only those behind the scenes knew the extent of the bitterness behind the breach. Mabel Collins was not less outspoken about the 'old lady', of whom she wrote:

She had a greater power over the weak and credulous, a greater capacity for making black appear white, a more ceaseless and insatiable hatred of those whom she thought to be her enemies, a greater disrespect for les convenances, a worse temper, a greater command of bad language, and a greater contempt for the intelligence of her fellow- beings than I had ever supposed possible to be contained in one person.'

And from my knowledge of her, this was no exaggeration.

This acrimonious power-struggle brought to light several aspects of Mabel's character that would otherwise have remained undetected. Like D'Onston himself, she had a dual personality. On the surface she was an elegant, beauti-

ABOVE York Terrace, Regent's Park – where Mabel Collins lived. Her belief in magic led her to be ensnared by D'Onston

fully gowned lady of fashion. Intelligent, charming and captivating, she seemed to be above all crudities and lusts. In reality she was quite capable of indulging her uninhibited, unrestrained sexual passions in whatever manner amused and excited her. Today such things are easily understood, even if frowned on a little, but in her time these drives had to be kept as private as state secrets. Even her affair with D'Onston had to be masked as a business relationship.

When we understand this, we can see that Blavatsky's exposure of Mabel's sexual penchants was devastating, especially since charges of 'Tantrism' were involved. The Tantric teachings were originally crafted in India and the followers of these teachings were wedded to secrecy, but with time their secrets became known. They believed that it was possible with mantras and rites to appease, fascinate, bind, drive away, create enmity and even kill. Their doctrines justified the use of all aspects of life. This even involved the deliberate cultivating

> **She had a greater power over the weak and credulous, a greater capacity for making black appear white, a more ceaseless and insatiable hatred of those whom she thought to be her enemies**

of repulsive or frightening acts in order to prove that the adept was above fear and disgust. Put into practice this meant that the adept was encouraged to break taboos and allow the sexual drives free range. Group sex, sodomy, incest, bestiality and even necrophilia was acceptable in Tantrism. And now Mabel Collins was identified as accepting such doctrines.

The Blavatsky camp was not short of 'evidence' to throw at Mabel. It was noted that her story *The Idyll of the White Lotus* was based on a period when the Egyptian faith and priesthood '...had already begun to lose its purity and degenerate into a system of Tantric worship contaminated and defiled by black magic, unscrupulously used for selfish and immoral purposes.' Then Blavatsky herself stated that even Mabel's cherished *Light on the Path* contained dangerous teachings, 'whose Occult venom and close relationship to Tantrika Black magic has never been suspected by the innocent and sincere admirers of this otherwise priceless little book...' Then, for the first time, Theosophists

were told about Blavatsky's actions in taking over the authorship of the crucial chapters of *The Blossom and the Fruit*.

For Mabel Collins it was humiliating beyond belief to know that from then on the Society was free to picture her in her unbridled, private ecstasies. Her enemies were now able to talk of her indulgence in orgies and imagine her coupling with the traditional rutting goat of the Satanists. In desperation she started an action for libel against Blavatsky. This was lodged in July 1889 but did not reach court until July 1890. It was a very short-lived action; in the opening moments Blavatsky's attorney showed the counsel for Mabel Collins a letter written by Mabel. The action was halted immediately, but the contents of this letter were never disclosed. Had Mabel been indiscreet enough to actually record details of her sexual taboo-breaking? It seems very possible, and her vulnerability in this area makes it easy to understand why D'Onston could exercise such a control and hold over her.

Chapter 18

Tongue-Tied by Fear

Both Cremers and Mabel Collins were still angry and seething over Blavatsky's brutality and spitefulness when suddenly, the whole affair was completely overshadowed. Overnight their thoughts became focused on something far graver and much more menacing. This was a supreme turning-point in their lives, as Cremers tells us:

It was a month or so after this scene that an incident happened, fraught with tremendous consequence to all three of us in partnership in the Pompadour Cosmetique Company. It was Mabel Collins who first aroused suspicion in my mind that D'Onston was Jack the Ripper.

One morning she entered the office in Baker Street, and after a nervous glance round the place whispered, 'Where is he?'

'Out,' I replied. 'Why - do you want him?'

She shuddered. In her eyes was the shadow of a haunting fear. 'Vittoria,' she said, 'I believe D'Onston is Jack the Ripper.'

I looked at her in astonishment. 'You must be joking,' I said, but I could see that she was quite serious. 'What on earth makes you say that?' I asked.

'Something he said to me, Vittoria. Something he showed me. I cannot tell even you - but I know it Vittoria - and I am afraid.'

There was no doubt at all about that. Fear reflected in every expression of her eyes and in every shrinking gesture. It was, too, the first occasion on which I had heard the name of Jack the Ripper mentioned since that day in December 1888, when I entered the room at 17 Lansdowne Road, and saw Helena Blavatsky and the Keightleys, crouched over Lord Crawford's article in the Pall Mall Gazette. Since then the Ripper had passed almost entirely from my mind, until Mabel Collins blurted out her fears and suspicions to me.

You may wonder, as I have often wondered since, what it was that D'Onston said to Mabel Collins, or what it was he showed her, which made her so certain that he was Jack the Ripper.

We shall never know now, for she is long since dead. And she never confided in me, as she usually did about anything of great moment. She told me for example of D'Onston's shattered romance with Ada. And this, I should say, was the most intimate revelation he ever made to anyone regarding his private life. Mabel Collins did not hesitate to tell me this story of her lover, readily acknowledging that this inability to forget Ada was the cause of many quarrels between them.

Yet, for some strange reason only known to herself, Mabel Collins never dropped the slightest hint of what D'Onston had said or done to cause her to approach me with that expression of awful dread in her eyes, and say, 'Vittoria, I believe D'Onston is Jack the Ripper.' Consequently, the whole thing passed from my mind. At the time, I remember thinking that there might have been some misunderstanding between them, and that things would sort themselves out as they so often do under these circumstances. I thought no more about it.

But - there came a day when my own suspicions were awakened by an incident which occurred when I was alone with D'Onston in our office at Baker Street.

We were chatting together about nothing in particular when in a chance remark, he mentioned his wife. This was the first time I had ever heard of the existence of such a person. I had always regarded him as a hard-and-fast bachelor impervious to any emotional or romantic feeling. I pricked up my ears, but as he made no further reference to the lady, I felt impelled - despite my usual practice not to ask questions - to say casually, 'What happened to your wife, D'Onston?' Whether he sensed that it was no idle question in spite of the manner in which it had been asked, I know not. But I shall never forget the sudden change which came over him. He had been lounging in a chair, and we were talking quietly. But now - he rose to his feet and commenced pacing the room diagonally, from one corner to the other. Backwards and forwards he paced, an expression of restless uneasiness in his eyes. Then as he passed the desk at which I sat, he suddenly paused in his stride, faced me, and raising his head made a dramatic gesture across his throat with one finger.

It was just as though he were drawing a knife across it. At the same time he gave an unearthly guttural groan. Then he resumed his restless pacing, and as I covertly watched and saw him gain control over himself, there came to mind the spoken fear of Mabel Collins when she unburdened herself of her terrible suspicions.

'My God,' I thought, 'he is Jack the Ripper!'

The sinister throat-cutting gesture he made with his finger seemed to confirm what Mabel Collins had confided to me, and at once my brain began a process of speculation. When had D'Onston married, and where? Who was his wife? Had he in fact murdered her? If so, how had he managed to escape suspicion? These thoughts flooded my mind even as D'Onston continued to pace the office.

One could not murder with impunity without arousing some suspicion, I conjectured mentally; and yet - Jack the Ripper had. In fact, had he not murdered woman after woman and got away with it? There flashed through my mind the stories D'Onston had related revealing scant respect for human life. All this passed through my mind in a matter of seconds, but I knew better than to press for any further information regarding the fate of his wife. Instead, in a perfectly casual tone, I asked:

'Any children?'

'No, Vittoria,' with that mirthless smile. 'No encumbrances.' 'Father dead?'

'Yes - curse him!' This with a sudden startling vehemence.

In consequence of this second outburst, I decided to ask no more questions for the time being regarding D'Onston's family life; but in that moment there was born in me a determination to find out all I could about him. I became intent on piercing the aura of mystery with which he had enshrouded himself.

At the very first opportunity I told Mabel Collins of the incident in the office, and she nodded her head.

'Yes, Vittoria,' she said, 'I know he has been married, but he will never talk about his wife. I did not know that he had killed her. He simply said that she had disappeared suddenly - vanished completely, and he had not heard of her for years.'

It struck me at the time, how readily and without surprise Mabel Collins accepted the idea that her lover had murdered his wife. She then went on to express her dread of the man.

'Vittoria, I am terrified of him,' she declared. 'I know he is Jack the Ripper and I want to get *away from him, but I am afraid. He has such powers - I wish he would leave me alone - go away - do anything - only leave me alone. I would give him money - anything - if only I could be free of him...'*

I had never seen Mabel Collins in such a state of mind as this. Usually calm and equable of disposition, she was now in the throes of something approaching terror. I had of late noticed that the infatuation that once possessed her regarding D'Onston, had cooled; and this cooling of affection coincided with the day she came to me and declared, 'Vittoria, I believe D'Onston is Jack the Ripper.'

And now - here was I, a prey to those very same suspicions; equally convinced with Mabel Collins that D'Onston was indeed the mass murderer of the East End. I no longer felt governed by the thought that if I was destined to acquire knowledge it would come to me without seeking. I was determined to probe the secret of D'Onston's origin and satisfy myself of his identity with Jack the Ripper.

I only know that some inner force urged me on. Something compelled me in this matter. I know not what. I was in no hurry, and was prepared to bide my time. And then as if to impress upon me the urgency of my quest, another incident occurred.

Mabel Collins came to my flat late one evening. It was clear that she was in great distress. Her eyes were swollen with weeping, and she looked positively ill. I brewed some tea, and when she had recovered to some extent, she said:

'I'm leaving D'Onston, Vittoria, I cannot stand it any longer, he terrifies me - I must get away from him, or I shall go mad - I am afraid of him Vittoria, I cannot tell you anything - but I want you to help me.'

She paused to get her breath while I poured her out another cup of tea. She drank it eagerly, and then went on:

'I have made arrangements to go to Scarborough and stay for a few months. Nobody but you will know where I am Vittoria, and - I want you to promise that on no account will you let D'Onston know where I am. Promise me Vittoria.'

'Of course I promise you,' I replied, at the same time remarking that I thought she was making too much of a small thing.

'But you don't know, Vittoria,' she insisted, her eyes pleading for some understanding of her plight. 'You don't know him as I do.'

'I'm very glad I don't if this is the state he can reduce one to,' I retorted, adding: 'Well - you get away to the East Coast as soon as you can and forget everything. Otherwise I can see you heading for a nervous breakdown. Let me know when you are settled, and write me poste restante. Then you can be sure your letters will not be intercepted.'

Just as she was leaving me later that evening, I noticed that she walked hurriedly past the room occupied by D'Onston. And then as she bade me goodbye at the door, she whispered to me: 'He is Jack the Ripper, Vittoria.'

I did not know how she knew. I had an idea that one day, later on perhaps, when she got over her fear, she might tell me of her own accord; but that day was never to come, as it happened, for reasons which I shall explain later.

Since Mabel never fully confided in Cremers, what possible fears could have kept her from unburdening herself? The answer lies in her complete acceptance of magical illusions. She really believed in D'Onston's imaginary powers. She really feared the working out of curses. If she was ritually sworn to secrecy, then she would feel herself tongue-tied and helpless to denounce him. He would be mockingly amused to allow her to label him as the Ripper. There was no danger in that, no one would take her mere assertion seriously. Yet the evidence that had devastated her had to be protected. This was only given to her after she had been terrified into accepting it. Her tongue was then stilled by threats of Satanic retribution. Her superstitious frame of mind made her an easy, pliable victim. A frame of mind that made her impotent, and her own worst enemy.

BELOW
Baker Street in the 1800's

Chapter 19

The Doubts Vanish

Vittoria Cremers' devotion to Mabel Collins was based on much more than homage to intellect. In truth she was in love with the romantic novelist; and this lesbian passion now led to a sudden breach between them. It was a breach cruelly and coldly engineered by D'Onston in a spirit of vengeance, as Cremers reveals:

Mabel Collins went to Scarborough as intended, and from time to time I received letters from her. Meanwhile D'Onston had taken her departure with a singular lack of interest.

'So Mabel's gone?' was all he said, and never mentioned her name again for several days. And then one afternoon, he drifted into the office.

At this time the Pompadour Cosmetique Company was not in a very flourishing condition, and as neither D'Onston nor Mabel Collins appeared to be very interested in it, I decided to wind things up and get out of town for a while. I was in the process of sorting out some papers when D'Onston entered the office in his usual soundless way. He perched himself on the table, and I told him what I proposed doing.

'I quite understand Vittoria,' he said; and then in quiet, unimpassioned tones he began to tell me certain things about Mabel Collins. What they were does not matter. They were of a purely personal nature, and had nothing whatever to do with the Ripper story. They related to details known only to Mabel Collins and myself so that I felt very angry when I realized that D'Onston could only have derived the particulars mentioned from Mabel Collins herself.

That same night I wrote off to Scarborough, repeating what D'Onston had told me. I asked Mabel Collins for any reasonable explanation of her conduct, and informed her that if none was forthcoming then our friendship must cease.

I was hopeful that she would be able to justify her breach of confidence in some way, and awaited her reply with some little anxiety. A day or so later, her reply came. In it she simply said that she 'quite understood'. There was not a word of apology or explanation, no denial, no excuse; nothing but the acknowledgment that she 'quite understood'.

It was a sad moment for me, and I felt a blaze of anger against D'Onston. I called him into the office and told him that he was a swine to have betrayed a woman who had been so kind to him. But he simply smiled that smile which was always so irritatingly expressionless.

It was this attitude on his part which filled me with such disgust, that, in my determination to discover who and what he was, I resorted to a course which, otherwise I should never have entertained. I fully realized that in other circumstances it would have been a low-down thing to do; but, his treatment of Mabel Collins and our suspicions that he was Jack the Ripper, seemed at the time, to justify me in what I did.

I had previously noticed that whenever he went out, he always locked the door of his room. This excited no wonder in my mind, because other people were living in the house. I had also noticed, on the few occasions I entered the room - always when he was present - a black enamelled deed-box as one sees in a solicitor's office. More than once in fact I knocked my shin against it, on one occasion remarking to D'Onston, 'What on earth have you got in that box?'

'A few first editions, Vittoria' he replied, adding, 'Books are very heavy, you know. I also keep some of my private papers in it.'

It was the recollection of this latter remark, which determined me to find out what really was in that box. 'Private papers,' he said, and I wondered whether those papers might yield any clue to his identity, or provide any other information of interest. Both Mabel and I were certain that D'Onston was not his real name, and Mabel Collins once told me that he 'claimed relationship with the Roslyns'. But who the 'Roslyns' were she knew not.

'I have tried all manner of ways to find out who he is,' she once told me when we were discussing the mystery. 'I have tried to trap him into betraying himself. But he is too damned clever, Vittoria - too cunning.' From time to time, when he went out, I entered his room by means of a key which I had found on an old bunch I always kept. I tried all the smaller keys on this same bunch on the two locks with which the box was secured. They did not fit. I went to another neighbourhood and scoured second-hand shops for old keys, and at length discovered one that fitted.

Armed with this, I seized the opportunity when D'Onston was out, and entered his room. In a few minutes I was on my knees beside the open box, carefully lifting from it the books he had mentioned. I noticed that they were all to do with Magic, one or two of them being written in French. Had I known what I know now I would have looked to see whether the recently published book by Eliphas Levi was among them, but I did not take note of any of the authors. Nor was I particularly interested in the books. It was his 'private papers' that intrigued me, to see what light they might throw upon D'Onston or his family.

But there was not a single paper or document to be seen. Nothing but the books I have mentioned and which I removed with great care so that I could replace them exactly as I found them. Nothing that is, but a few ready-made black ties of the old-fashioned sort that were very popular in that day. These had the knot already tied, with a kind of slot at the back through which one pushed the loose end after placing it round one's collar.

They were the kind that D'Onston always wore.

Frankly I was very disappointed with the results of my burglarious venture. I had hoped for something more informative than those sombre articles of men's wear. Chancing to lift one out of the box, I could not help observe that it was a grubby-looking specimen altogether. I was just about to replace it, when - something caught my eye.

On the underneath side of the flowing end of the tie, and also at the back of the knot, I saw a dull sort of stain. I examined it more closely, and discovered that where the stain was, the tie was quite hard as though something had congealed upon it. I picked up another one, and on the underneath side of this one I found a similar stain. I examined the others (I do not remember how many), and in each case found a stain. There were no marks on the outer side of the ties beyond what might have been a smear of something.

I felt completely baffled by my discovery. I could not imagine what the stains could be; nor how they came to be in such a peculiar position; above all - why did D'Onston keep the filthy, dirty things which he could not wear again anyway?

D'Onston, himself, was to supply the answer to these questions at a near future date, but, meantime - I was still as far off as ever from finding out anything about him from the mysterious black-enamelled tin box which I had ransacked.

Chapter 20

Confirmed by Confession

In 1890, the Westminster Gazette raised the spectre of the Ripper once more. In its July report it claimed that the police had gained advance information about the killer's intentions. A new cycle of horror was about to begin. Cremers read this and decided to mention it to D'Onston to gauge his reaction. But he was one step ahead of her. At the office, he waved the very paper at her while ridiculing the report. Then his mood changed abruptly. 'There will be no more murders.' He strode across to Cremers' desk and leaning over it, stared down at her and said, 'Did I ever tell you that I knew Jack the Ripper?'

When recalling this incident, Cremers wrote:

I felt a cold shudder run through me. Anxious to gain time to recover myself, I bent down and opened a drawer. 'Where the deuce did I put that ruler?' I muttered to myself, and continued to fumble in the drawer. But D'Onston was apparently not to be denied, for still leaning over the desk he repeated: 'Did I ever tell you that I knew Jack the Ripper?'

Cremers was now disturbed and uneasy but she struggled to stay calm and gave a noncommittal reply. At that, D'Onston began to pace up and down the room. Cremers was reminded of the time when he'd mimed the throat-cutting of his wife. And then, in a quiet voice D'Onston said:

'You know that when Mabel first wrote to me, I was in hospital? That was just after the last of the murders, Vittoria,' he went on, 'and you can take it from me that there were no more Ripper murders after that one in Miller's Court on November 9.'

He paused for a moment, came close to me, and then remarked that he was living in the Whitechapel neighbourhood at the time. I never thought to inquire where, nor to ask him why he was residing in such a squalid district. It simply did not occur to me, but my brain registered the fact that he was living in the murder area at the time of the crimes.

D'Onston went on to say that he was taken seriously ill and had to enter hospital. Something to do with the 'Chinese slug', was how he put it to me and then he explained:

'It was there that I met him, Vittoria. He was one of the surgeons who operated, and of course when he learned that I had also been a doctor he became more interested in my case, and we became very chummy.

'Naturally we talked about the murders, because they were the one topic of conversation. One night he opened up and confessed that he was Jack the Ripper. At first I did not believe him, but when he began to describe just how he had carried out the crimes I realised that he was speaking from actual knowledge, and - was speaking the truth.'

D'Onston rose from his chair and recommenced his restless pacing up and down the room. Then once more he paused and stood before me.

'At the inquest, Vittoria, it was suggested that the women had been murdered by a left-handed man, or at any rate with the left hand.' He smiled in derision. 'It just shows that they could not see an inch before their noses, Vittoria. My surgeon friend explained exactly how the medical witnesses fell into this error. He also told me that he always selected the place where he intended to murder the women. It was for a very special reason, Vittoria, which you would not understand. He took the Whitechapel Road as a sort of base for his operations, and made several journeys before deciding on the spots best suited to fit in with his scheme of things. Then, having got his victims to these particular places, he manoeuvred to get behind them.'

At this point D'Onston paused for some seconds which seemed like hours to me. He seemed as though he were reliving something that had happened some time before. Then he spoke again.

'All those doctor fellows took it for granted that Jack the Ripper was standing in front of the women when he drew the knife across their throats,' he said, and paused again before continuing, 'but he wasn't, Vittoria - he wasn't. He was standing behind them like this.'

As he spoke D'Onston crossed over and stood behind my chair. And even at this length of time, I can still recall the uncanny expectant feeling I experienced as I sensed him standing there behind me. I could almost feel a knife at my throat.

But he was talking again, quite calmly, yet with deadly earnestness. 'It was quite simple really,' came his voice from behind as he reached round and placed his left hand over my mouth and nose, pulling my head back. I could scarcely breathe so firm was his grasp. Then his other arm reached round my neck from the right, and again he spoke.

'You see Vittoria,' he said, 'this arm (waving his right arm before my eyes) would be quite free, and all my friend had to do was to make one quick slash with his knife, and it was all over before they could utter a sound.'

As he said this, D'Onston's arm relaxed and he withdrew it from my neck. At the same time he lifted his left hand from my nose and mouth, and I drew a deep and grateful breath. He continued:

'At the inquests, Vittoria, these same doctors made a point of mentioning that the women did not fall but appeared to have been lain down. This is about the only thing right about their evidence. They did not fall. My friend did lay them down, and then - when they were on the ground he carried out the mutilations - so.'

As he spoke he came round to the front of me and made a gesture with his thumb. I remember it striking me at the time - although I must admit to being too shocked to observe very clearly - that the motion was in the form of a downward triangle, such as I had often seen him making upon the door of his room on more than, one occasion. Meanwhile D'Onston was continuing his narrative of what, he said, happened at the scene of the crimes:

'Everybody, Vittoria, including the police were on the look-out for a man with bloodstained cloth-ing,' he said, 'but of course, killing the women from behind, my doctor friend avoided this, as their bodies offered some sort of protection. Had he been in front of them his clothes must have been drenched with blood. Once or twice, he told me, he foun d a spot or two, but soon removed them.'

All D'Onston's revelations were made in a detached fashion; a mood which persisted, even when he revelled in the details of the gory knife-work. Cremers was appalled:

For the first time, I learned how, in two instances, the murderer, after mutilating the bodies, took away the uterus; the mere mention of this fact horrified me, but I can see now the lifeless grin D'Onston gave when relating this part of the story. I was still more horrified when he went on to say:

'He tucked these organs in the space between his shirt and tie, Vittoria,' going through the motions as he did so. I could not repress a shuddering 'Good God!' as, in a flash, there came to my mind the recollection of that black tin box in D'Onston's room containing the ties with their stained underparts. At the time I rifled that box and came upon them, I had wondered why on earth lie kept such filthy neckwear, and how they had become stained in such an unlikely spot.

Now I knew! D'Onston had, out of his own mouth, provided the only explanation. From his own lips he had not only explained how those stains could possibly have come upon the underside of his ties, but had also revealed that they came from the blood of his murdered victims.

All this passed through my mind in a flash as I took in the purport of his story; and in that moment one question dominated my mind. 'Who but the murderer himself could possibly know the things D'Onston had told me?'

It was borne in upon me that the 'doctor friend' referred to was nothing more than a figment of D'Onston's imagination, invented to conceal his own identity with Jack the Ripper. I was now convinced beyond all doubt that the man standing before me was in fact the Whitechapel murderer, and that Mabel Collins' fears of her lover were well founded.

During the latter part of his narrative I had been careful to intently watch him. I noticed that the expression on his face never changed except for that one momentary grin when he described the removal of the uterus. Never once did he falter in his recital which was spoken in quiet, unemotional tones. At the end he looked intently at me to see how I was taking it. I endeavoured to assume a calm demeanour; and, to break the spell, as it were, I asked:

'But what did your friend want D'Onston? What was he after?' By this time, I was more than ever anxious to get right into the mind of the man I now regarded as a self-confessed murderer. I was puzzled at the idea of this apparently serene-minded, cultured person, as I knew D'Onston to be, being guilty of the horrors he had just described to me without the quiver of an eyelid. I had not read about the crimes at the time, and it was not until this moment, and from D'Onston himself, that I learned

the nature of the atrocities. Hence my desire to discover the motive which impelled him to such grue-some crimes. Why had he murdered so many women, and what was the object of the ghastly mutila-tions inflicted upon his victims after death?

There was no thought in my mind of any Magical background to the murders. I knew little of Magic beyond Mabel Collins' description of D'Onston as a great Magician'. It was the recollection of the ties and his explanation of how they had become stained with blood, which prompted me to ask him, 'But what did he want. What was he after?'

D'Onston was not to be drawn, however. He simply shrugged his shoulders as he answered: 'He did tell me, Vittoria, but you would not understand.'

I knew it would be fruitless to pursue the question, so I next ventured: 'But didn't you ever tell the police?'

He smiled. 'Yes,' he replied. 'I told them all right, but by the time they went to arrest him he had gone. You know, Vittoria, the police were awful duffers. Why, they had me in for questioning on two occasions, but of course I was easily able to satisfy them and they had to let me go.'

I proceeded to ask him a question here and there, giving no inkling of my suspicions. Yet, all the time I was paving the way towards a scheme, whereby I hoped to persuade him to set down in fuller detail (with the object of newspaper publication) the story of his mysterious 'doctor friend'. I have already mentioned that I knew he was invariably hard up, and now that Mabel Collins had broken with him, and there was very little coming in from the Cosmetique Company, I felt sure he must be worse off than ever.

Suddenly I put my scheme to him direct, pretending enthusiasm for the idea as though it had just struck me.

'You know D'Onston,' I said, 'that's one of the most amazing stories I have ever heard. There's money in it. Why don't you write it up for the Pall Mall Gazette? You are well in with Stead, and he would jump at it.'

'Oh, I don't know,' he began, and for the first time in my experience, it seemed as though he were not anxious to make money. But I kept at him.

'It would create a sensation,' I told him. 'It would pave the way for stories in other newspapers.' He still appeared to be reluctant, but I was determined to make him set down in black and white the ter-rible story he had told to me.

I got out pen and paper and placed them before him. D'Onston sat down and began to scribble off three or four pages of preamble, handing them to me to read as he did so. The perspiration simply poured from him as he wrote, and he was obviously labouring under some great emotional strain as he scribbled away. I had never before seen him so much affected. Suddenly he rose to his feet, roughly pushed back the chair, and them, quietly, and without a trace of the turmoil which had been so pronounced a few seconds before, he turned to me and said, 'I'll finish it tomorrow, Vittoria, and take it straight round to W. T. Stead in the morning.'

But I knew full well that he would do no such thing. The moment had passed. His excuse was simply a subterfuge to escape writing the story. I realized that he never intended to write it, but had been forced to fall in with my suggestion in order to lull any possible suspicions. I believe now that he knew I suspected him and was trying to elicit how much Mabel Collins had told me.

He left the office and entered his room taking with him the few sheets of paper on which he had begun to write his story.

At the time Cremers had no knowledge of the fact that WT. Stead already knew about D'Onston's yarn involving Dr Davies. Neither did she know that Stead himself suspected D'Onston of being the Ripper. But because she was certain that D'Onston would remain silent, and because she had such strong suspicions, why didn't she take her story to the police? This is something she dealt with forthrightly when she talked to O'Donnell, saying:

I am a Theosophist. I believe that whatever we do upon this planet we shall reap our deserts in the next incarnation. I believe that we shall be rewarded or punished according to our life on earth. It is not for me to interfere with the laws which govern destiny. I did not do it then, I would not do it now. You will remember that D'Onston had already assured me in the clearest possible terms that there would be no more Ripper murders and that the last one had been committed on 9 November, 1888. He had spoken truly. There were no Ripper murders during the twenty one months which had elapsed between that date and the time of our talk. Consequently I felt quite certain that, being the murderer, he knew what he was talking about. That there would be no more murders by Jack the Ripper. I knew there was no further danger to others.

Cremers' reasoning was sound. D'Onston's illness reduced him to a shadow of his former self. He was now a man of hints and threats and little more; while his so-called magical powers were not even potent enough to bind the three partners together. Inevitably their joint business ended in near farce.

Chapter 21

The Trio Split

Vittoria Cremers saw Mabel as a partner for the last time late in the summer of 1891. It was a brief meeting lasting just under an hour and it only came about because Mabel needed a great favour. D'Onston had a collection of letters from Mabel; compromising letters, so explicitly sexual that they gave him the power of blackmail. She knew where they were kept and even had a key that fitted the lock of the trunk that housed them. But she was far too terrified to enter his room and rifle the trunk, so she pleaded with Vittoria to recover the letters for her. Vittoria took pity on her, gamely extracted the letters and sent them on to Mabel's hideaway. It was some three weeks later before D'Onston discovered the loss of the letters, but he seemed to accept that Mabel herself could have returned to London and taken them. In fact Mabel had stupidly written to him and boasted that he no longer had a hold over her. In the same letter she ordered him out of his room and informed him that all his furniture would be taken away within days.

This marked the end of the Pompadour Company and its name and assets were taken over by a West End consortium. Mabel returned to York Terrace, Cremers went back to Mrs Heilmann's, while D'Onston took out a summons against Mabel demanding the return of the purloined letters. It seemed a foolish act to involve the courts, but D'Onston seemed blinded by hate and the action actually came to a hearing, as Cremers testifies:

*T*he case was heard at Marylebone, and I shall never forget the shock I had on seeing D'Onston. He looked terribly ill, and although he moved in the same silent manner when his name was called and he made his way to the witness-box, he seemed to lack the sanguine calm that was so usual with him. He was not exactly agitated - as he had been when writing the few pages describing his meeting with Jack the Ripper - but he struck me as being uneasy and not sure of himself.

Perhaps he had expected Mabel would have handed over the letters without daring to appeal in court. I don't know! But when he was asked to take the oath, I noticed that while his lips moved mouthing the words of the ordinary Christian oath sworn upon the New Testament as is usual, not a sound could be heard. Somehow, he must have satisfied the court usher, but although I was sitting not far away I could not hear even a whisper.

D'Onston was represented by a solicitor who asked him to tell the court in his own words the nature of his complaint against Mabel Collins.

He opened his mouth as though to speak, mumbled a few unintelligible words, and stopped, gazing blankly in front of him. It was incomprehensibly eerie to me, who had never found D'Onston at a loss for words. But now he was literally speechless. The solicitor had already outlined the case stating that 'the defendant broke into D'Onston's room and extracted private letters from a locked trunk'. And now, when D'Onston was being invited to substantiate this allegation, he became dumb. It was for all the world as if he were paralysed. The words simply refused to come, and after an interval during which his solicitor went across and spoke quietly to him, D'Onston left the witness-box and the solicitor announced that under the circumstances he could carry the matter no further. Whereupon the case was dismissed.

I left the court hurriedly without even waiting to say goodbye to Mabel Collins. I believed then that both she and D'Onston had passed from my life forever. It was true so far as Mabel Collins was concerned, for I never saw her again. But as regards D'Onston, I was wrong.

"D'Onston had a collection of letters from Mabel; compromising letters, so explicitly sexual that they gave him the power of blackmail"

Her very last contact with the man was charged with menace. D'Onston wrote to her asking for money and demanding to meet her on her own. She ignored the note but others followed. Finally she met him at midnight at her lodgings but took care to have two stalwart men waiting in a recess at the foot of the stairs. D'Onston must have caught sight of the men lurking in the dark alcove since he simply took the money offered him and left without even a word of abuse.

She felt it an anti-climax but often wondered what might have happened if her allies had not been on hand. Four years later Cremers returned to England after lengthy tours abroad. Awaiting her was a bundle of letters in D'Onston's handwriting, but she resisted the urge to open them and threw them into the fire. In later life she regretted this. What if they'd given further clues to his past and misdemeanours?

Vittoria Cremers died in 1936 without knowing D'Onston's real name and background and without realising just how invaluable her testimony would prove to be.

ABOVE
Compromising letters from Mabel to D'Onston were found

❝ I left the court hurriedly without even waiting to say goodbye to Mabel Collins. I believed then that both she and D'Onston had passed from my life forever. ❞

Chapter 22

Blood and Magic

Two different reasons for the murders are included in Vittoria Cremers' memoirs: according to the Earl of Crawford, Black Magic was at play; according to D'Onston, a twisted doctor was at work. Both explanations seem in conflict with each other and yet, as we shall see, there is no clash. We are merely looking at the two halves of one disclosure; both halves fashioned by one man alone. But if the key to the mystery lies in ritual murder then we need to understand fully the magical mentality of the Victorians.

A superficial or token appraisal is not enough. Only a deep and comprehensive study of their beliefs can show us why murder was enshrined in both White and Black Magic. This does not mean that the ceremonies of the believers unleashed genuine powers. On the contrary, all magical claims are nonsensical. This tragic belief in magic is a burden inherited from the childhood of Man. It is a retrograde view of the Universe and of Man himself. It gains force by using childish dreads and yearnings. It adds to these uncertainties its special heady symbolism and its language of spurious wisdom. All magic deludes by promising unrealizable control; by offering entry into halls of hidden and terrible knowledge. In its most menacing forms it succeeds only by twisting the minds of its dupes, but never by violating the laws of nature. Where it does succeed, this is simply because its devotees have acted out their fantasies, for even the direst nonsense can become a force when peobearded scholar who dresses in splendid robes and wields a heavy, ornate baton. He is also a Queen's Coroner for North London. His name is Dr Wynn Westcott. In recent years some wild fantasists have named him as Jack the Ripper! But this is worthy of a yawn and no more. What is worth noting, though, is his status and the fact that surrounding him were people of intellect, all committed to the belief that they could control people and events by means of signs, symbols, chants and the power of their magically charged wills.

In time the Golden Dawn would count among its members Arthur Machen, Maude Gonne, Florence Farr, Mrs Oscar Wilde, Algernon Blackwood, Sir William Crookes, and W. B. Yeats. Its members would take oaths which threatened them if they disclosed the 'great secrets', declaiming such nonsense as: '...submitting myself by my own consent to a deadly stream of Power, set in motion by the Divine Guardians of this Order, living in the Light of their perfect justice, who can, as tradition and experience affirm strike the breaker of the magical Obligation with death or palsy, or overwhelm him with misfortunes...'

These, remember, were the beliefs of those who labelled themselves as

ple believe in it. So exactly what were the strange beliefs of our forbearers? Beliefs that are even now nurtured by some.

The year is 1888, year of the Ripper. In a London hall a small body of men and women gather to found the Isis-Urania Temple of the Hermetic Society of the Golden Dawn. It is a magical order devoted to so-called White rituals and its Supreme Magus is a solemn-faced,

'Whites'; those whose powers were alleged to be used for the good of mankind. But did these White beliefs go as far as to condone murder for the common good? They certainly did. The supreme example of a-'magical murderess' can be found in the person of Dr Anna Kingsford, a strong influence on Samuel Mathers, one of the founders of the Golden Dawn, and friend of Wynn Wescott.

Anna Kingsford was a doctor of medicine who developed a fanatical hatred of all who practised vivisection. Top of her list of these vile practitioners' were three Frenchmen: Claude Bernard, Paul Bert and Louis Pasteur. She absorbed the antique magical belief that one could 'kill by willing'; a belief that she found confirmed by the sixteenth century magician Paracelsus:

It is possible that my spirit, without the help of my body, may through a fiery will alone, and without a sword, stab and wound others. It is possible for me to bring my adversary's spirit into an image, then double him up and lame him at pleasure...

In Dr Kingsford's case she targeted Claude Bernard as the foremost living representative of the 'vivisection conspirators' and with passionate energy invoked the wrath of God upon him. She later said that she felt as if she had been transformed into a spiritual thunderbolt at the moment of her curse. Shortly afterwards she heard the news of the death of Bernard and was so overwhelmed by her imagined victory that she almost swooned. Then in an ecstatic mood she proclaimed, 'Woe be to the torturers. God willing, what a murrain there shall be among them! I will make it dangerous, nay deadly, to be a vivisector.' And in that state she began to will the death of Paul Bert.

Her diary for 12 November 1885 records:

Yesterday, November 11, at eleven at night, I knew that my will had smitten another vivisector! Ah, but this man has cost me more toil than his master, the fiend Claude Bernard. For months I have been working to encompass the death of Paul Bert, and have but just succeeded. But I have succeeded, the demonstration of the power is complete. The will can and does kill... Now only one remains on hand - Pasteur, who is certainly doomed.. I have killed Paul Bert, as I killed Claude

Bernard; as I will kill Louis Pasteur, and after him the whole tribe of vivisectors...

She was then led to conclude that, 'The White Magician is authorized to undertake an act of execution in the same spirit and with the same motive, and in the same frame of mind, as he would entertain in the act of destroying a noxious beast or a venomous reptile or creeping things.'

If you consider that such a creed was held by a cultured lady who styled herself a Christian, then it easy to see that an avowed Satanist would have no problems at all in endorsing murder as a worthwhile pursuit. Indeed Eliphas Levi, the French occultist who influenced D'Onston, Kingsford, Blavatsky, and Wescott wrote:

Black Magic is really only a graduated combination of sacrileges and murders designed for the permanent perversion of the human will and for the realization in a living man of the hideous phantom of the demon... The rites of Black Magic have remained revolting like the impious worships it produced... There was always the same passion for darkness; there were the same profanations, the same sanguinary processes. Anarchic Magic is the cultus of death. The sorcerer devotes himself to fatality, abjures reason, renounces the hope of immortality, and then sacrifices children. Fie forswears marriage and is given over to barren debauch. On such conditions he enjoys the plenitude of his mania, is made drunk with iniquity till he believes that evil is impotent and, converting his hallucinations into reality, he thinks that his mastery has power to evoke at pleasure all death and Hades.

Among the self-proclaimed 'elite' drawn to such magical thinking was a Robert Stephenson from Hull. This was a name which would have meant nothing to Cremers, or Mabel Collins. Yet it was their partner's name. A name which now gives us access to many archives and their myriad secrets.

Chapter 23

Man of Secrets

My first verdict on the Whitechapel mystery was an open one. None of the contending theories stood up to close scrutiny, so the killer was probably someone unknown and unsuspected. Study of the FBI material on serial killers led to a slight alteration in emphasis: the killer could have been suspected at one time but may well have been able to give a convincing display of total innocence. Then, using the documents of the time and coupling these with our present-day understanding of the serial sexual killer, I was able to draw up a comprehensive profile of the man.

This, in turn, could be realistically reduced to thirteen essential points. The final Master Profile read:

He will not be a person of stature, importance, or fame; however:

1. He will be fit, agile, with an icy control; but at the same time will be inclined to be taunting.
2. Not physically distinguished. Neither a giant nor a dwarf.
3. Nothing about him to repel or arouse suspicion.
4. Able to talk easily with prostitutes.
5. He will have an intimate knowledge of the area.
6. Either still living in the area, or having a retreat there, i.e. a club, institute, friend's or relative's place.
7. Not a surgeon, but with some limited medical knowledge. Maybe a one-time assistant to a GP, or former medical student.
8. Possibly enjoying some form of cover.
9. Possible past record of deviancy. Perhaps even interviewed by the police of the day.
10. May have talked about the killings.
11. A careful planner, but a high-risk taker.
12. His motives? Perverted sexuality.
13. His career ended by death, disablement or leaving the country.

No previous Ripper author had ever taken Roslyn D'Onston seriously; the man had since dismissed out of hand as a Walter Mitty character. This dismissal arose from blunders made in 1975. D'Onston's birth certificate showed that his father was a 'seed crusher' of Charles Street, Sculcoates. This wrongly interpreted. His place of birth was described as a humble one, while his father was pictured as a mere working man toiling in a mill. This, naturally, was at complete odds with D'Onston's claims to have come from a well-off family whose money had allowed him to study in Paris and Munich. So the man became a liar of no importance. His colourful tales of soldiering with Garibaldi, of travels in India and more, were all written off as sheer moonshine. One visit to Hull changed all that.

Records at Hull showed the address at Charles Street to have been a large middle class town house. As for the father, he actually *owned* the mills where the seeds were crushed. He was in fact, co-proprietor of the firm of Dawber and Stephenson, bone and seed crushers and linseed oil manufacturers. The mother in turn was from another mill-owning family, the Dawbers. So, it was clear that the Stephensons had ample money, as

LEFT A study of the FBI material on serial killers led to a slight alteration in emphasis

> " The killer could have been suspected at one time but may well have been able to give a convincing display of total innocence. "

D'Onston had claimed. And there were other discoveries which showed that D'Onston had a past that simply cried out for full examination.

An autobiographical article of his was located, containing oblique clues of missing years of his life. He spoke of holding a post under the Crown. This was the starting point for a process of gradual elimination which finally led to the discovery of his service records. He was found to have been a customs officer. And there, in those records, was proof of his early entanglements with prostitutes, and proof of his deviancy. Other discoveries came to light. Each one tying the man into the Ripper killings. For the first time ever there emerged an authentic candidate who came to fit the master profile to perfection.

He was born on 20 April 1841 and baptized as Robert D'Onston Stephenson. As a schoolboy he set out to control people and events and believed that he'd found a way through the agency of magic. Of that period he wrote 'I was always...fond of everything pertaining to mysticism, astrology, witchcraft, and what is commonly known as "occult science" generally; and I devoured with avidity every book or tale that I could get hold of having reference to these arts.' None of this study ever gave him the control he wanted and he stayed frustrated until he tried hypnotism. He recalled: 'I remember, at the early age of fourteen, practising mesmerism on several of my schoolfellows, particularly on my cousin, .a year younger than myself. But on this boy ...developing a decided talent for somnambulism, and nearly killing himself in one of his nocturnal rambles, my experiments in that direction were brought to an untimely close.'

In his teens he took rooms in Munich and studied chemistry under the renowned Dr James Allan, a Scotsman who had been the former right-hand assistant to Baron Liebig. From there he went on to Paris for further studies in medicine and while there began to revive his old passions:

...my interest in the effects of mind upon matter once more awoke, and my physiological studies and researches were accompanied by psychological experiments. I read Lytton's Zanoni at this time with great zest, but I am afraid with very little understanding, and longed excessively to know its author; little dreaming that I should one day be the pupil of the great Magist, Bulwer Lytton - the one man in modern times for whom all systems of ancient and modern magism and magic, white or black, held back no secrets.

A chance meeting in Paris put an end to his excessive longings. In 1859 he met Bulwer Lytton's son and young Lytton took to D'Onston and willingly furnished him with an introduction to his great father. In the following spring D'Onston met Sir Edward in London and was greeted warmly. D'Onston records: 'I suppose Sir Edward was attracted to me partly by my irrepressible hero-worship of which he was the object, and partly because he saw that I possessed a cool, logical brain, had iron nerve, and above all, was genuinely, terribly in earnest.'

After a brief period D'Onston won complete acceptance. Sir Edward summoned him to a private meeting-place and there began his training. D'Onston wrote:

I entered, he was standing in the middle of the sacred pentagon, which he had drawn on the floor with red chalk, and holding in his extended right arm the baguette, which was pointed towards me. Standing thus, he asked me if I had duly considered the matter and had decided to enter upon the course. I replied that my mind was made up. He then and there administered to me the oaths of the neophyte of the Hermetic lodge of Alexandria — the oaths of obedience and secrecy.

In later years D'Onston divulged little of the actions of his lodge but he did speak of '...the books of "Black Magic" I had studied under Lytton. Hermetics have to *know* all the practices of the

ZANONI.

BY

THE AUTHOR OF "NIGHT AND MORNING," "RIENZI," ETC.

"In short, I could make neither head nor tail on't."
Le Comte de Gabalis.

IN THREE VOLUMES.
VOL. I.

LONDON:
SAUNDERS & OTLEY, CONDUIT STREET
1842.

ABOVE Zanoni, the 1842 novel by Edward Bulwer-Lytton

"forbidden art" to enable them to overcome the devilish machinations of its professors.' He must have revelled in writing those hypocrital words, for one thing is certain; in all of his known writings of the nineteenth century there is not a single Christian sentiment. Blood, death, necromancy and deception are his constant themes. Compassion, charity, humanity, arc themes always absent.

His initiation provided the first great excitement of the year 1860, then came an unexpected distraction. Like many other reckless, bright-eyed students, he was ensnared by the fire and fury of Garibaldi's rising. In Britain Garibaldi's admirers set out to raise a foreign legion to fight in Italy, but in order not to fall foul of the law they called the legionnaires 'Excursionists'.

From his home in Hull D'Onston offered his services, then he came south to London, stayed at an old school friend's house in Islington and made a second application. This time he inflated his age to twenty-two, in order to escape a veto from his father, and with a background of some military training, became a lieutenant in the Southern Army of Italy. There were no non-combatants in that army. Those with medical training simply swapped their swords for scalpels as the need arose. It was then that D'Onston gained the experience in crude surgery, handling wounds and amputations that only military campaigns provided. Then it was down scalpel and battle order once more. Sword in hand, D'Onston killed and maimed legitimately on the battlefields of Italy. At a totally impressionable age, he became hardened to the sight of blood, death and mutilation. Edward Bowra, one of his colleagues and far less hardened, wrote this of the campaign:

> Only when we came to charge bayonets and form line.. .would they retreat. And it was well for them that they did so, for so awfully excited and enraged were we that I do not believe we would have given any quarter or spared a single soul. You cannot imagine with what a fierce exulting pleasure, I received with my comrades the order to charge bayonets and clear the ditch. I was heartily ashamed of myself a few hours afterwards...for having allowed such animal and barbarous passions to get the better of me...

Some men, though, treasured the barbarous passions and D'Onston was one

❝ Only his magical studies fired his dreams and gave promise of tingling excitements and revelations ❞

of these. But could such passions arouse thoughts of sexual slaughter? Given the right circumstances, such a transition is certain. The whole history of brutal warfare is marked by sexual atrocities. Indeed, a smiling British mercenary with the Croat army recently said this: 'I've always wanted to kill legally...I have that feeling to take people out. I've always wondered what were going through, like, Yorkshire Ripper...Black Panther's mind. These had no compassion. They had no feeling. I want this feeling... it's like higher than any drug can get you...'

In D'Onston's case the drug of slaughter was quickly withdrawn. After a victorious few months the conflict was over and a return to England replaced the rough comradeship with infantile student carousing and passive medical studies. For him it was empty and arid. Only his magical studies fired his dreams and gave promise of tingling excitements and revelations. His restless demanded action, so he threw aside his books and set off for the west coast of Africa. There was the lure of the unknown and the chance to view the wonders wrought by witch-doctors. And

there, in Africa, he killed his first woman, a fact that he coldly put into print twenty-eight years later. But this was only an interlude; a foolhardy, vagabond existence, hardly likely to meet with family approval. When his funds ran out his family put him under pressure and he returned home, reluctantly, rebelliously. In March 1863 he took up a safe, predictable post at the Customs House in Hull. It was a post he came to treat with contempt: 'almost a sinecure', he termed it. And his records show that he gradually antagonised his superior officers. This was to be expected; after all, in his own eyes, he was naturally superior to all the manikins around him, whatever rank they held.

By 1867 his father was not only a prominent manufacturer but held the elected post of Collector of Hull Corporation Dues - a post equivalent to City Treasurer. His elder brother Richard was now a ship-owner, partner in the firm of Rayner, Stephenson and Co., Vice-Consul for Uruguay and a Hull City councillor. Yet not all his considerable family influence could shield him from Nemesis. The reckoning came at last in 1868.

Chapter 24

Reveal and Conceal

At this point our documentary sources begin to intermesh even more closely. The Cremers' memoirs; the service records and D'Onston's own writings, all tell of the same sets of events, and yet there are differences. How then do we evaluate these differences? What standards do we adopt to sort out the evasions from the revelations? Let us take Cremers' writings first. In her case we can show that she has remarkable powers of recall. Many of the things she records can be confirmed from documents she had never seen; documents that, in fact, were not available for public scrutiny until the 1970s. Foremost among these documents are those in the Scotland Yard files directly involving D'Onston.

In D'Onston's writings we meet a very different state of affairs. Here we have to realize that there are complications due to the ancient standards he admired and adopted. These were esoteric traditions that left him free to mingle straightforward truth with parables or illuminating fiction. This is precisely the attitude adopted by his great hero and mentor Lord Lytton who said of his *Zanoni*:

'It is a romance, and it is not a romance. It is a truth for those who can comprehend it, and an extravagance for those who cannot.' Of this same book he said also: 'I love it not the less because it has been little understood, and superficially judged by the common herd. It was not meant for them. I love it not the more, because it has found enthusiastic favourers amongst the Few.'

❝ It is a romance, and it is not a romance.
It is a truth for those who can comprehend it,
and an extravagance for those who cannot ❞

The same stance was adopted by Mabel Collins who said of her *Light On The Path*: 'The whole...is written in astral cipher, and can therefore only be deciphered by one who reads astrally.' Blavatsky endorsed this view saying: '...only students with spiritual discrimination will most likely discern between symbolic statements, imaginative superstructure and actual facts'. D'Onston gave clear warning that he worked with these ideas in mind. In his *Pall Mall* article 'Obeeyahism (African Magic) he promised that he would go further into the subject in a forthcoming book:

Sube, the Obeeyah, a work of professed fiction. Its readers will have to decide for themselves how much is absolute matter of fact - whether all or none — and how much imagination. It will not be my part to give any clue to the student of occultism; it may convey many new ideas, and indicate the true lines on which his investigations should proceed; to the holiday maker and the simple novel reader it will certainly give a fresh and hitherto unexperienced sensation...

Forewarned is forearmed. We can now put to one side those writings of his which are self-evidently esoteric; that leaves us with a group of articles which refer to real events of his life. Even these have to be treated with caution since the need to reveal has been tempered by the necessity to conceal, by carefully matching all the known writings we can eliminate the misleading passages in his testimony and so grasp the truth.

A document of prime importance was located first of all in the 1931 edition of *Man's Survival After Death* by the Rev. Charles Tweedale. This turned out to be defective and a further search led to the original complete text of 1892. This had appeared in *W. T. Stead's Review of Reviews* (New Year's Extra Number). The authentic, full account read:

DEAD OR ALIVE

Mr. R. D'Onston sends me the following communication:

'To those instances in Real Ghost Stories of ghosts who have kept promises made in life to appear to those dear to them, may I add my own experience?

The incident occurred to me some years ago, and all the details can be substantiated. The date was August 26th, 1867, at midnight. I was then residing in the neighbourhood of Hull, and held an appointment under the Crown which necessitated my repairing thither every day for a few hours' duty. My berth was almost a sinecure; and I had been for some time engaged to a young North-country heiress, it being understood that on our marriage I should take her name and "stand for the county", or rather for one of its divisions.

'For her sake I had to break off a love affair, not of the most reputable order, with a girl in Hull. I will call her Louise. She was young, beautiful, and devoted to me. On the night of the 26th August we took our last walk together, and a few minutes before midnight paused on a wooden bridge running across a kind of canal, locally termed the "drain". We paused on the bridge, listening to the swirling current against the wooden piles and waiting for the stroke of midnight to part forever. In the few minutes' interval site repeated, sotto voce, Longfellow's Bridge, the words of which, "I stood on the bridge at midnight", seemed terribly appropriate. After nearly twenty-five years I can never hear that piece repeated without feeling a deathly chill and the whole scene of two souls in agony again rising before me. Well! midnight struck, and we parted; but Louise said: "Grant me one favour, the only one that I shall ever ask you on this earth, promise to meet me here twelve months tonight at this same hour." I demurred at first, thinking it would be bad for both of us, and only re-open partially healed wounds. At last, however, I consented, saying: "Well, I will come if I am alive!" but she said, "Say alive or dead!" I said, "Very well then, we will meet, dead or alive."

'The next year I was on the spot a few minutes before the time; and, punctual to the stroke of midnight, Louise arrived. By this time, I had begun to regret the arrangement I had made; but it was of too solemn a nature to be put aside. I therefore kept the appointment, but said that I did not care to renew the compact. Louise, however, persuaded me to renew it for one more year, and I consented, much against my will; and we again left each other repeating the same formula, "Dead or alive".

'The next year after that passed rapidly for me until the first week in July, when I was shot dangerously in the thigh by a fisherman named Thomas Piles, of Hull, a reputed smuggler. A party of four of us had hired his 10 ton yawl to go yachting round the Yorkshire coast, and amuse ourselves by shooting sea-birds amongst the millions of them at Flamborough Head. The third or fourth day out I was shot in the right thigh by the skipper Piles; and the day after, one and a quarter ounce of No. 2 shot were cut there from by the coastguard surgeon at Bridlington Quay (whose name I forget for the moment), assisted by Dr. Alexander Mackay, at the Black Lion Hotel. The affair was in all the papers at the time, about a column of it appearing in the Eastern Morning News, of Hull.

'As soon as I was able to be removed (two or three weeks) I was taken home, where Dr. Kelburne King, of Hull, attended me. The day — and the night - (the 26th August) came. I was then unable to walk without crutches, and that for only a short distance, so had to be wheeled about in a Bath chair. The distance to the trysting being rather long, and the time and circumstances being very peculiar, I did not avail myself of the services of my usual attendant, but specially retained an old servant of the family, who frequently did confidential commissions for me, and who knew Miss Louise well. We set forth "without beat of drum", and arrived at the bridge about a few minutes to midnight. I remember that it was a brilliant starlight night, but I do not think that there was any moon, at all events, at that hour. "Old Bob", as he was always affectionately called, wheeled me to the bridge, helped me out of the Bath chair, and gave me my crutch. I walked on to the bridge, and leaned my back against the white painted top rail, then lighted my briar-root, and had a comfortable smoke.

'I was very much annoyed that I had allowed myself to be persuaded to come a second time, and determined to tell "Louise" positively that this should be the last meeting. Besides, now, I did not consider it fair to Miss K., with whom I was again negotiating, en rapport to a certain extent. So, if anything, it was in rather a sulky frame of mind that I awaited Louise. Just as the quarters before the hour began to chime I distinctly heard the "clink, clink" of the little brass heels, which she always wore, sounding on the long flagged causeway, leading for 200 yards up to the bridge. As she got nearer I could see her pass lamp after lamp in rapid succession, while the strokes of the large clock at Hull resounded through the still night.

'At last the patter, patter of the tiny feet sounded on the woodwork of the bridge, and I saw her distinctly pass under the lamp at the farther end — it was only twenty yards wide, and I stood under the lamp at my side. When she got close to me I saw that she had neither hat nor cape on, and concluded that she had taken a cab to the farther end of the flagged causeway, and (it being a very warm night) had left her wraps in the cab, and for purposes of effect had come the short distance in evening dress.

'"Clink, clink" went the brass heels, and she seemed about passing me, when I, suddenly urged by an impulse of affection, stretched out my arms to receive her. She passed through them, intangible, impalpable, and as she looked at me I distinctly saw her lips move, and form the words, "Dead or alive". I even heard the words, but not with my outward ears, with something else, some other sense - what, I know not. I felt startled, surprised, but not afraid, until a moment afterwards, when I felt, but could not see, some other presence following her. I could feel, though I could not hear, the heavy, clumsy "thud" of feet following her; and my blood seemed turned to ice. Recovering myself with an effort, I shouted out to "Old Bob" who was safely ensconced with the Bath chair in a nook out of sight round the corner. "Bob, who passed you just now?" In an instant the old Yorkshireman was by my side "Ne'er a one passed me, sir!" "Nonsense, Bob," I replied, "I told you that I was coming to meet Miss Louise, and she just passed me on the bridge, and must have passed you, because there's nowhere else she could go! You don't mean to tell me you didn't see her?" The old man replied solemnly, "Maister Ros, there's something uncanny about it. I heard her come on the bridge, and off it, I'd know them clicketty heels anywhere; but I'm dommed, sir, if she passed me. I'm thinking we'd better gang." And "gang" we did; and it was the small hours of the morning (getting daylight) before we left off talking over the affair and went to bed.

'The next day I made inquiries from Louise's family about her, and ascertained that she had died in Liverpool three months previously, being apparently delirious for a few hours before her death, and our parting compact evidently weighing on her mind, as she kept repeating "Dead or Alive! Shall I be there?" to the utter bewilderment of her friends, who could not divine her meaning, being, of course entirely unaware of our agreement.'

> " Suddenly urged by an impulse of affection, stretched out my arms to receive her. She passed through them, intangible, impalpable, and as she looked at me I distinctly saw her lips move, and form the words, 'Dead or alive'. "

This one article on its own gives us great insight into his thinking. We can now see that the accounts related by him to Cremers have been rejigged to conceal his true background. For reasons of his own he needed to keep his activities in Hull as secret as possible. Perhaps he had primitive loyalties to some members of his family. One thing is certain, his need to talk about his past later came to overwhelm his caution, and many enigmas now become transparent. He *had* held a military rank, but not in the British army. The ...jaunts with some brother officers...' were with fellow Customs Officers, not army men. The events that put him in a bath-chair were not the result of the death of his loved one but involved a suspicious shooting affair. The phantom footsteps on the bridge were heard in Hull, not in London. What then *can* we believe in this account? Surprisingly the answer is: everything. When first re-searched though, many things failed to find support. The claim about his post was true, but his service records showed no mention of the grave shooting incident. And the Hull newspapers printed no reports either, though logically the event should have made front page. All very puzzling. But the doubts were resolved when misplaced service papers came to light. There, in the records for 26 August 1868 is confirmation: '...Mr Stephenson accidentally received a gunshot wound, which quite incapacitated him for duty... ' (this referred back to 7 July). Spurred by this, new searches were made in the newspapers, but their columns held no records. The area of search was then broadened until finally, my colleague Andy Aliffe, focused his tired eyes on a gem of a report. Weary days spent peering at microfilm had paid off. The find was the 16 July issue of the *Bridlington-Quay Observer*, and it carried this text:

SERIOUS ACCIDENT TO A HULL GENTLEMAN

*O*n Tuesday afternoon, Mr. R. D'O. Stephenson, of Her Majesty's Customs, at Hull, while cruising off Flamborough, on board the yacht Flying Scud, met with a serious accident. The party on board were shooting sea birds, and Mr. Stephenson was standing just abaft the mast, waiting for a shot, when a boatman belonging to the yacht, who was behind him, took up one of the guns to fire, and managed to explode it prematurely, sending the whole charge into the back of Mr. Stephenson's thigh. The heavy charge (1.25 oz of No. 2 shot), at a distance of about two yards, tore a jagged hole, about 1.5 inches wide, and the same depth, and lodged itself in a lump near the bone, which, however, it miraculously failed to injure. Fortunately a gentleman was on board who had had some surgical experience, and immediately applied temporary bandages. The unfortunate gentleman was landed at Flamborough as soon as possible, and carried to the top of the cliffs by a stalwart young fisherman. The only available conveyance being a fish-cart, belonging to the landlord of the inn, it was filled with clean straw, and the patient removed in it to Bridlington, where, under the skilful hands of Drs. Brett and Mackay, the greater part of the shot was removed. We are informed by eye witnesses that the sang-froid with which the sufferer treated his terrible and painful wound was something remarkable, and excited the warmest admiration and sympathy in the bystanders. We understand that there is every hope of saving the limb, provided that neither erysipelas nor gangrene (the two great dangers in gun-shot wounds) make their appearance. Mr. Edwin Gray, timber merchant, Hull, very kindly superintended the landing at Flamborough.

A second report in the *Bridlington Free Press* for July 11 confirmed that the surgical aid was given at the Black Lion Hotel. So every verifiable detail stood up, even to the size and weight of the lead shot. Given the extent of his injuries it became easy to see that the phantom footfalls on the bridge were simply night sounds hallucinated into a ghostly experience. When operating on his thigh, the surgeon would have made free with his injections of pain-killing morphia. In that year, as articles in the *Practitioner* show, doctors held that there were no dangers involving in injecting morphia, even over long periods. So the drug

ABOVE North landing, Flamborough Head, c. 1880

would have been a D'Onston's daily disposal during his recovery. His capacity for hallucinating was thus at a peak.

Remarkably the Bridlington reporter confirms the observations made by others in later years. They all noted D'Onston's icy control. This reporter drew special attention to D'Onston's coolness, cold-bloodiness, *sangfroid*, when coping with his terrible injury. This is the Ripper of my profile.

One mystery still remains though. Why did the Hull papers ignore the story, for D'Onston's recollection is here at fault? The only sensible explanation seems to be that the story was hushed up. Family pressure may have been strong enough to have achieved this, especially since one of the leading papers was owned by a branch of the Stephensons.

There were pressing reasons for avoiding any type of scandal at that time, for the Stephenson family were still desperately trying to save the proposed alliance with the heiress. D'Onston's conduct, on the other hand, had gradually placed their well-laid plans in dire jeopardy. And 1868 had already been crises-ridden from its very first months.

Chapter 25

The Death of Love

Before D'Onston became utterly corrupted he suffered from a peculiarly Victorian malady. He believed that he could redeem a prostitute by the sheer force of love. Novelist George Gissing, a fellow Yorkshireman, also suffered from this malady. In Gissing's case he threw away his academic future by stealing from the men's locker rooms in Owens College. None of these thefts were for personal gain, they were desperate attempts to provide a prostitute with money and wean her away from the streets. He adored this girl, Nell Harrison, and after a term of imprisonment and wanderings in America, Gissing actually married her. The union was a disaster. The girl proved to be a shrew, unable to meet his standards and she drifted back to the streets, leaving Gissing drained and desolate. D'Onston too staked everything on an idealized union between himself and a prostitute. This was the girl he called Ada-Louise'; the girl of his hallucinations; the one he was forced to reject.

Naturally, a woman of the streets was quite unacceptable to his family and he knew this; yet, in his determined, egocentric fashion he intended to push through with his plans. But the family was able to enforce its will after D'Onston ran up huge gambling debts. His father agreed to pay off the debts on condition that all contact with this street-woman ended. D'Onston gave in and promised to break with Ada-Louise, but secretly he arranged a poignant once-a-year tryst with her. And there may well have been some extra meetings, for on 25 February 1868 he was warned that the heiress had found out about this love-affair, '...not of a most reputable order...' as he put it. He dealt with this crisis by taking unauthorized leave and was summoned to face an internal disciplinary hearing by the Customs.

Records of this hearing show how a letter was involved that could have seriously affected his prospects and character, if not dealt with at once. The Hull disciplinary board seemed quite happy to accept this generalized statement, but the London HQ insisted in knowing more. The Hull Collector then reported; '...his absence was caused by information given to him that certain matters prejudicial to his moral character had been communicated to the lady he is about to marry, and it was of great importance to his future welfare, that he should at once refute them.'

But things had now gone too far. His excuses failed to placate the lady and the marriage hopes were ended. From then on it was a downwards track. He began seeking comfort from the dockside ladies of pleasure and for his pains contracted a venereal disease which left him in a feverish state.

The official report on his condition states '...there is little or no doubt that the illness from which he is now suffering is the result of the discreditable life he leads.' And while he was still on sick leave, came the shooting incident; an event which must have raised serious doubts about his reliability. There were many boats available for hire in the area, but D'Onston had opted for one owned by a man with a reputation as a smuggler. That man had then shot him. An accident it was said, but was it?

What on earth was a Customs Officer doing in the company of such a man? Was this smuggler benefiting from inside knowledge of Customs plans? Was this wounding the result of a quarrel between knaves? Or were gambling debts involved?

Whatever the Hull Customs discovered about this shooting is still unknown - the records are infuriatingly incomplete, but on his return to duty he was dismissed from the Service: 'Struck off the establishment' is the official wording. This in itself was a severe disgrace and a blow to his prominent family with its aura of respectability. What is more this dismissal raised doubts about his basic honesty and stability. It even hinted at criminality.

Shortly after this ignominy he left Hull for London and covered up all traces of his past life as a servant of the Crown. From now on, his hometown was linked with sorrow and failure. And most tragic of all for him, it was dark-shadowed by the death of the only woman he would ever love. A death which he would always blame on the profession of harlotry. But for that stigma, he would have unfailingly made her his wife. Instead, all the love within him died with her. In later years the harlots themselves would pay for the cruel death of his last streak of humanity. In the meantime, he hit back at his family and its respectability by marrying his mother's illiterate servant girl.

His marriage to this Anne Deary took place on 14 February 1876 in the North London Church of St James in Holloway. Ironically it was in this very same church that Frederick George Abberline was married. The two men may even have known each other at this time, since D'Onston worked as a journalist

for one of the papers covering the district, and Abbeline worked and lived in the same area until 1873 when fate first took him to Whitechapel.

D'Onston's marriage certificate has an added significance since it shows his first known use of *Roslyn* as a forename. This use marks a new stage in his thinking. It is an open avowal of his dedication to magic, for the name has Rosicrucian and occult Masonic origins. And to understand fully the importance of such a name-change we have to look again at the Victorian hermetic traditions. These traditions held that allegories, even single words, had powers of their own and became channels of esoteric communication. This may sound high-flown and foolish to us, but here our own reactions are of little account. What matters is that believers in such teachings were influenced, moved and energized by these ideas. There are many examples to prove this but just two will be enough.

Take the case of George Russell. He came to write and paint under the name *AE,* and when he did so, it was as if a secondary personality took over control. But his *AE* is not a display of initials, as most people thought, it is short for 'AEon', a mystic Gnostic name; the name, in fact, of the solar-phallic God of the Gnostics. It was a name that he swore had been whispered to him in a vision. As with D'Onston's choice it was heavy with sexual symbolism. So it is hardly startling to find that Russell, like D'Onston, felt himself drawn to forbidden rites:

> I was one of the Children of Light...I became aware of a dark presence beside me, and I trembled because I knew it was one of the Children of Darkness. But this being whispered gently to me, 'We of the Darkness are more ancient than you of the Light', and at the saying of that, I forsook my allegiance to the Light, and my whole being yearned to lose itself in that Divine Darkness.

At this time Russell was a member of the Hermetic Society in Dublin along with W. B. Yeats, who, on joining the Golden Dawn, showed signs of the same duality of thought by taking this magical motto for himself: 'Demon Est Deus Inversus' (The Devil is the Reverse Side of God).

This was a motto that D'Onston himself could have easily found apt and acceptable, but in picking 'Roslyn' he had chosen a name that in a way foreshadowed his future; its Rosicrucian echoes spoke of a cross and a five-petalled rose. In the warped traditions dear to him the five-petalled rose came to stand for Babylon, the Scarlet Woman, the Great Whore.

Once again, these ideas may seem infantile and hard to take seriously, yet we have to disregard such judgments, and recognize that what is *real* for the believer is the only thing that matters. Illusions, fantasies, hoaxes and misconceptions can all lead to real life actions, for better or worse. In D'Onston's case his illusions even led him to make a gruelling journey through India in search of real magic. He was then thirty-seven.

In 1896 D'Onston wrote a full account of these experiences in India. His journeying took place in 1878, at a time when Bulwer Lytton's son, Edward held the post of Viceroy of India. The old friendship with Edward (begun in

BELOW Rosy Cross of the Golden Dawn

> " There is some evidence in police files, though, that at one point realism overtook dreaming "

Paris), stood him in good stead. Many doors opened for D'Onston and in the company of several high-ranking army officers he witnessed a fantastic display of 'real magic' invoked by a wealthy diamond merchant, Mr Jacob of Simla.

He saw a barren walking-stick put out green shoots, then twigs and branches which burst into flowers, which then in turn changed into bunches of fine black grapes; and this was only the beginning. Next, he took part in a ceremony which culminated in a sword being thrust right through his body. He felt not the slightest pain. After that the whole company were treated to an amazing series of visions including a re-run of the Charge of the Light Brigade. The entertainment ended when Mr Jacob waved a wand and summoned up thousands of butterflies from the air.

When his account of these wonders was first published, D'Onston was written off as a second Baron Munchausen. His stories were branded 'tall tales'. But within months, the scoffers had to eat their words. Mr Jacob of Simla was still alive and in an interview published in *Borderland* in 1897 he testified that D'Onston's visit *had* taken place and his narrative was substantially correct.

Having said that, Mr Jacob then confessed that he had cleverly staged a series of tricks to deceive D'Onston and the others. It had all been done with the greatest of skill and Mr Jacob even disclosed some of the secrets lying behind his elegant illusions. The rod that had blossomed was a specially prepared stick. The sword was driven through at a safe place, only after much pinching had left the flesh bloodless and numb. It was a trick worked daily by many showmen in India. The rest of his magical act Mr Jacob preferred to keep secret.

Three points of importance arise out of these reminiscences of India. We can see that D'Onston was driven to great lengths by his beliefs; we can prove that his writings were extremely accurate; and we can note that despite his experience, he readily accepted skilled trickery as proof of the paranormal. In short he was both gullible and open to massive self-deception. This is a dangerous combination for any man; in his case the danger grew to deadly proportions.

Until the Ripper terror opens we can only chart many stages of D'Onston's life in a sketchy manner. His callous ventures in America in the 1870s can be found only in Cremers' all-too-brief account. Yet everything we can glean about him points to a steady decline in his fortunes. It wasn't poverty, at first. He simply became more and more of a loner, his brain tormented by delusions of grandeur which were fired by drugs and drink; and his unshakeable belief in the power of magic.

Set in his mind was the eternal dream, that one day he would make the great breakthrough. Then, his knowledge of the occult would change his fortunes and status and astonish the sheep-like masses.

There is some evidence in police files, though, that at one point realism overtook dreaming. Belatedly, D'Onston once made a totally different bid for status. He was even prepared to discard all Bohemian ways and commit himself to a regular, responsible post. Ironically, it was a post serving, and controlled by, the police. In July 1886 the Secretaryship of the Metropolitan and City Police Orphanage fell vacant and was advertised. The salary was £200 a year, but the successful candidates had to give security for the sum of £500. Among the candidates was Roslyn D'Onston. The man who remained convinced of his own intellectual superiority was not even shortlisted. Had he reached that list he would have found himself face to face with Sir Charles Warren, who chaired the selection board. Had he been chosen, the Whitechapel murders would never have happened: the post offered long-term stability and recognition; it also involved living over the orphanage at Wellesley House in Twickenham - far from the dark alleys and slum rooms and hideaways of the East End. The post went to Arthur Kestin, a respectable managing clerk, the sort of man D'Onston would despise. D'Onston could only see this rejection as a personal affront - he had no means of knowing that the post had attracted 372 candidates. He put all thoughts of conformity behind him and resigned himself to an increasingly vagabond existence and the seamy pleasures of the East End. From then on there was only one obstacle in his way - his wife.

Chapter 26

Sacrificial Rites

D'Onston's wife is a woman of mystery. We know where she came from. We know she once served as personal maid to D'Onston's mother in Hull. We know where she married, and when. And we know that she was still alive in 1886. And there our knowledge ends. Here we need to refer back to Cremers' testimony. She has told us that she knew of the wife's existence only through a chance remark made by D'Onston. It was after this, that Mabel Collins revealed that as far as she knew, the wife had 'disappeared suddenly - vanished completely'. But Cremers drew a very different conclusion. She had questioned D'Onston about his wife, but he had never given a straight answer. Instead he reeled as from an emotional shock. His agitation at that time; his pacing about the room, his throat-cutting gesture; led her to accept that the wife had been killed by him.

Cremers could not have checked on the story; to search she needed D'Onston's full name. But even that name would have yielded nothing. The records are mute. All our searches have failed to find a death certificate for Mrs Stephenson. What we can find, though, are reports in 1887 of the discovery of various parts of a dismembered woman's body in the Thames and the Regent's Canal.

The first find was of a trunk section floating near the Thames ferry landing at Rainham in Essex. These remains were thought to be those of a woman aged about twenty-eight or -nine; later

ABOVE The entrance to the Regent's Canal at Limehouse, 1823

on, the age was revised upwards. This horror of 11 May, was followed by five further finds in June, first came the discovery of a thigh in the Thames, near Temple Steps; then two arms and two legs were fished out of the St Mary's Lock section of the Regent's Canal. The body had been dissected with knife and saw by someone 'having a knowledge of a human body' - this was the conclusion of Dr Edwin Calloway. Although this corpse was never identified, it was the body of a woman who had never been a mother. The head, that might have provided important clues, was never found. So, could this butchered woman have been D'Onston's childless wife; the woman he 'killed' in his mime show?

All we know for certain, on this score, is that D'Onston was very familiar with the Regent's Canal. He had lodged just yards away from it in 1860; then in later years had actually lived near it; and visited two mission houses on the very edges of the canal. This was an ideal dumping spot for D'Onston if he wished to dispose of a dissected corpse. Remember, the canal fed south into the Regent's Dock, which in turn opened up into the Thames itself.

One other fact is worth noting; after these discoveries and the final inquest in August, D'Onston began to describe himself as 'unmarried'. *And this signifies that he knew that his wife was not going to return.* At this point he could afford to be both complacent and blatant, since the investigation into the identity of the body was never taken any further. This was the result of the inquest jury returning a quirky verdict of 'insufficient evidence to show cause of death'.

What we do know for certain is that shortly after his wife's vanishing act, D'Onston changed his life-style and — quite out of character — deserted London. Very strange. Since 1869, he'd been virtually ensnared by London. Even after trips abroad he'd always returned to the capital. It was always his home base; first in Holloway, then in different parts of the East End. Now he turned his back on the old haunts and delights, to take up residence in Brighton, in Black Lion Square, as a boarder at The Cricketers Inn. There he described himself as 'unmarried', 'single', but never as a 'widower'; though that description would have won him sympathy.

So why did he change? Was it because the secure post at the police orphanage had eluded him. Was this the final blow that led to a massive crisis of confidence? After all, he was forty five and all his cherished, magical rituals had failed him utterly. Was this enough to impel him to try something stronger, and push him into *advanced* Satanic practices? Were his victims doomed by his infantile need to revenge his lost love?

We now know that serial killers will go to extreme lengths to make their fantasies come true. Careful prior planning is one of the hallmarks of such killers, and in D'Onston's case we now have evidence of his bizarre, calculated moves. We can now show how he engineered a safe bolt-hole for himself right in the heart of Whitechapel.

In 1888 Brighton was renowned as a supreme place for rest-cures in its own right. As the *Penny Illustrated Paper* put it in its 21 January 1888 issue:

> *Are you suffering from 'the blues', down with 'the dumps', afflicted with 'vapours', neuralgia, rheumatism, pains in the back, or tic doloreuzx? Then, try my prescription! Go in for a Brighton Brightener! Remember that many a time and oft when it's foggy and gloomy in town, the Sun shines gaily in Brighton, chasing away Dull Care, and infusing some of the salubrious sparkle of good champagne into your and veins.... A Brighton Brightener! Elixir of Life! The dose for longevity and vigour!....*

Clearly, an ideal place to rest. But for those wanting special care and comfort in Brighton could also offer its outstandingly fine Royal Sussex Country Hospital, sited in a place where the fresh country air circulated day and with private bed could be secured in these ideal surroundings by anyone with money. It was the perfect place for someone seeking tranquillity. Given that understanding, consider this strange state of affairs. It is July 1888, D'Onston is living there in Brighton, just minutes from the seafront, when he suddenly puts on an act that he is suffering from neurasthenia. Now this describes a state of *excitability* and should not be confused with neurasthenia, it's very opposite. The treatment for neurasthenia was simple: a light diet, plenty of rest, no stimulants, and *fresh air*. In other words: a rest-cure. It was the perfect condition for a Brighton-based treatment. So in all logic D'Onston should have stayed put; that is, if there *had been* anything wrong with him.

Instead, he left Brighton and chose to go to the London Hospital in Whitechapel, with its grim reputation of pain and death. There, on 26 July 1888 he booked into a private bed, registered as a neurasthenic and began his rest-cure. Illogically, he chose to breathe the acrid, sooty, sulphur-laden was air of the East End, for month after month after month. His complaint was certainly faked. The symptoms: excitability, tension, sleeplessness, are easy to assume or induce. And this man, with his medical training, knew a great deal about inducing bodily reactions.

Once inside, with his aristocratic bearing and his private bed, he is privileged and uncircumscribed. He has ample time to prepare. First he needs to make himself 'invisible'. This is easily done, simply by being seen around often and everywhere. At all hours he can be spotted slowly walking the corridors and the grounds; pausing to talk to surgeons, physicians, orderlies, anyone he meets up with. In a short while he is accepted as that nice, mild-mannered man, who is ever restless; who finds it hard to sleep; who paces wearily around in order to become quite fatigued. Nocturnal prowling on his part becomes accepted as unremarkable, even expected; like those nocturnal excursions of Elephant Man, who was there at the very same time. But, at no point does D'Onston display any energetic movements. His swiftness of foot, his innate agility has to be disguised – at all times.

❝ We can now see that this letter was one of the utmost cunning. He has a need to talk about the murders ❞

In 1888 the grounds of the London Hospital were extensive, they were also dotted around with temporary huts and sheds left over from the erecting of a nurses' home and the enlargement of the medical college in 1887. At the side of the west wing was the large House Governors garden; to the rear was a huge open garden field. Around the perimeter mature trees and bushes abounded. For the most part, simple railings set in low brick walls surrounded the hospital grounds and its college. These could be easily scaled in seconds by anyone with agility and determination. With the greenery as quick cover, entry and exit was an easy matter. This made the hospital an ideal staging-post for D'Onston's series of premeditated killings.

His first killing was staged just two minutes' walk from the hospital entrance. The second was to the northwest of the hospital, but still within easy walking distance. The third was to the south-west of the building, roughly the same distance away as the second. The Mitre Square murder was the one most distant; but for someone in a hurry, still within quick reach of the hospital.

The Kelly murder was in a class of its own. The four others were quick 'taunt and display' killings; Kelly's was meant to be the peak of visual horror, and a leisurely indulgence in rituals of the blackest hate. The butchery was concealed within the privacy of a house, so an exit could be made at any time. No need to rush along back streets to the hospital. The return to base could be taken at a brisk walk. And, as always, the hospital grounds provided plenty of cover for a clean-up, even a change of clothing if needed.

D'Onston's stay at the hospital ended on Friday 7 December 1888, his 'rest-cure' had lasted a remarkable 134 days. But while in the hospital he had written two intriguing pieces: one a letter, the other a newspaper article. These were used as smokescreens, meant to mislead by diverting any suspicion away from him. By being obvious he hoped to be ignored. The letter came first. It was sent by him to the City of London Police on 16 October 1888. It read:

Sir, Having read Sir Charles Warren's Circular in yesterdays papers that 'It is not known That There is any dialect or language in which The word Jews is spelt Juwes.'

I beg to inform you That The word written by the murderer does exist in a European language, Though it was not Juwes.

Try it in script – Thus,
The Juwes. &c

Now place a dot over The Third upstroke (which dot was naturally overlooked by lantern light) and we get, plainly The Juives which, I need not tell you, is the French word for Jews.

The murderer unconsciously reverted, for a moment, To his native language.

Pardon my presuming to suggest That There are Three parts indubitably shown (2 another, probably) by the inscription.

1. *The man was a Frenchman.*
2. *He had resided a long time in Eng land To write so correctly;*

Frenchmen being, notoriously, The Worst linguists in the World.

3. *He has frequented The East End for years, to have acquired, as in The sentences written, a purely East End idiom.*
4. *It is probable (not certain) That he is a notorious Jew-hater: Though he may only have written it To Throw a false scent.*

May I request an acknowledgment That This letter has safely reached you, & That it be preserved until I am well enough to do myself The honour to call upon you personally.

I am Sir,
Yr. Obedt. Servant Roslyn D'O. Stephenson
PS. I can tell you, from a French book, a use made of the organ in question - 'd'une femme prostituee, which has not yet been suggested, if you think it worthwhile. R.D'O.S.

We can now see that this letter was one of the utmost cunning. He has a need to talk about the murders, but he is taking the precaution of shielding himself from too close a scrutiny. He creates a shield by first giving advance notice of a newspaper piece he has in mind. Then he gives the false impression that he is an invalid, scarcely mobile, who will call upon them when he is 'well enough'. This man has no intention of letting his conceit endanger him; his instinct for self-preservation is far too powerful to allow the hunt to centre on him.

The article, he then had in mind, appeared after the last victim was chosen and despatched. It was the strangest of all the accounts of the day. Its slant was new. But was it more than pure fantasy?

Chapter 27

The Veil Lifts

From the comfort of his hospital bed D'Onston had put together the article that had begun to germinate in his mind in October. It appeared on the 1 December 1888, on the front page of W. T. Stead's *Pall Mall* Gazette. It was a masterpiece of deception designed to make the author look both like a genius and a wild extravagant theorist simultaneously. Its lengthy title read:

THE WHITECHAPEL DEMON'S NATIONALITY:
AND WHY HE COMMITTED THE MURDERS.

In calmly reviewing the whole chain of facts connected with these daring and bloodthirsty atrocities, the first thing which strikes one is the fact that the murderer was kind enough to (so to speak) leave his card with the Mitre-square victim. But this most important clue to his identity, which 'he who runs may read', seems to have baffled the combined intellects of all grades of the police. This admits of no question, because we find in all the journals a note from Sir C. Warren to the effect that 'no language or dialogue is known in which the word "Jews" is spelt "Juwes".'

O! most sapient conclusion! Let us see what we can make of the word.

It will be remembered that a chalk inscription (which it is not denied was written by the mur-

derer) was found on the wall in Mitre-square, just above the body of the murdered woman. It ran as follows: 'The Juwes are the men who will not be blamed for nothing', and was evidently intended to throw suspicion on the Jews. This writing was seen by the police by means of artificial light, and was unfortunately obliterated by them before daylight. Hinc illae lachrymae!

Why did the murderer spell the word Jews 'Juwes'? Was it that he was an uneducated Englishman who did not know how to spell the word; was he in reality an ignorant Jew, reckless of consequences and glorying in his deeds; or was he a foreigner, well accustomed to the English language, but who in the tremendous hurry of the moment unconsciously wrote the fatal word in his native tongue?

The answers to these three queries, on which the whole matter rests, are easy. Juwes is a much too difficult word for an uneducated man to evolve on the spur of the moment, as any philologist will allow. Any ignorant Jew capable of spelling the rest of the sentence as correctly as he did, would know, certainly, how to spell the name of his own people. Therefore, only the last proposition remains, which we shall now show, in the most conclusive manner, to be the truth.

To critically examine an inscription of this kind, the first thing we naturally do is not to rest satisfied with reading it in print, but to make, as nearly as we can, a facsimile of it in script, thus:-

Juwes

Inspection at once shows us, then, that a dot has been overlooked by the constable who copied it, as might easily occur, especially if it were placed at some distance, after the manner of foreigners.

Juives

Therefore we place a dot above the third upstroke in the word Juwes, and we find it to be Juives, which is the French word for Jews. Strictly Juives and grammatically speaking, of course, it is the feminine form of Juijs and means 'Jewesses.' But in practice it will be found that (Frenchmen being notoriously the worst linguists in the world) most Frenchmen who are not either litterateurs or men of science are very inaccurate as to their genders. And almost all the ouvrier and a large majority of the bourgeois class use the feminine where the word should be masculine. Even the Emperor Napoleon III was a great sinner in this respect, as his voluminous correspondence amply shows.

Therefore, it is evident that the native language - or, to be more accurate, the language in which this murderer thinks - is French.

The murderer is, therefore, a Frenchman.

It may here be argued that both Swiss and Belgians make French almost their mother tongue; but Flemish is the natural and usual vehicle for the latter, while the idiosyncrasy of both those nationalities is adverse to this class of crime.

On the contrary, in France, the murdering of prostitutes has long been practised, and has been considered to be almost peculiarly a French crime.

Again, the grammatical construction of the sentence under examination is distinctly French in two points - first, in the double negative contained; and, secondly, in the employment of the definite article before the second noun. An Englishman or an American would have said, 'The Jews are men who, &c.' But the murderer followed his native idiom 'Les Juifs sont des hommes' in his thoughts, and when putting it into English rendered des hommes 'the men'.

Again, neither Belgians nor Swiss entertain any animosity to the Jews, whereas the hatred of the French proletarian to them is notorious.

The ground for research being thus cleared and narrowed, the next question is, what is the motive? Speculation has been rife, the cries are many; almost every man one meets, who is competent to form an opinion, having a different one.

And in endeavouring to sift a mystery like this one cannot afford to throw aside any theory, however extravagant, without careful examination, because the truth might, after all, lie in the most unlikely one.

There seems to be no doubt that the murderer, whether mad or not, had a distinct motive in his mutilations; but one possible theory of that motive has never yet been suggested. In the nineteenth century, with all its enlightenment, it would seem absurd, were it not that superstition dies hard, and some of its votaries do undoubtedly to this day practise unholy rites.

Now, in one of the books by the great modern occultist who wrote under the nom de plume of 'Eliphaz Levy', 'Le Dogme et Rituel de la Haute Magie,' we find the most elaborate directions for working magical spells of all kinds. The second volume has a chapter on Necromancy, or black magic, which the author justly denounces as a profanation. Black magic employs the agencies of evil spirits and demons, instead of the beneficent spirits directed by the adepts of la haute magie. At the same time he gives the clearest and fullest details of the necessary steps for evocation by this means, and it is in the list of substances prescribed as absolutely necessary to success that we find the link which joins modern French necromancy with the quest of the East-end murderer. These substances are in themselves horrible, and difficult to procure. They can only be obtained by means of the most appalling crimes, of which murder and mutilation of the dead are the least heinous. Among them are strips of the skin of a suicide, nails from a murderer's gallows, candles made from human fat, the head of a black cat which has been fed forty days on human flesh, the horns of a goat which has been made the instrument of an infamous capital crime, and a preparation made from a certain portion of the body of a harlot. This last point is insisted upon as essential and it was this extraordinary fact that first drew my attention to the possible connection of the murderer with the black art.

Further, in the practice of evocation the sacrifice of human victims was a necessary part of the process, and the profanation of the cross and other emblems usually considered sacred was also enjoined. In this connection it will be well to remember one most extraordinary and unparalleled circumstance in the commission of the Whitechapel murders, and a thing which could not by any possibility have been brought about fortuitously. Leaving out the last murder, committed indoors, which was most probably not committed by the fiend of whom we speak, we find that the sites of the murders, six in number, form a perfect cross. That is to say, a line ruled from No. 3 to No. 6, on a map having the murder sites marked and numbered, passes exactly through Nos. 1 and 2, while the cross arms are accurately formed by a line from No. 4 to 5. The seventh, or Dorset-street murder, does not fall within either of these lines, and there is nothing to connect it with the others except the mutilations. But the mutilations in this latter case were evidently not made by anyone having the practical knowledge of the knife and the position of the respective organs which was exhibited in the other six cases, and also in the mutilated trunk found in the new police-buildings, which was probably the first of the series of murders, and was committed somewhere on the lines of the cross, the body being removed at the time. Did the murderer, then, designing to offer the mystic number of seven human sacrifices in the form of a cross - a form which he intended to profane - deliberately pick out beforehand on a map the places in which he would offer them to his infernal deity of murder? If not, surely these six coincidences are the most marvellous event of our time.

To those persons to whom this theory may seem somewhat farfetched, we would merely remark that the French book referred to was only published a few years ago; that thousands of copies were sold; that societies have been formed for the study and practice of its teachings and philosophy; and, finally, that within the last twelve months an English edition has been issued. In all things history repeats itself and the superstitions of yesterday become the creeds of today.

" For the space of twelve months the inhabitants of the town had been in a state of wild panic at the periodical repetition of such hideous and objectless crimes "

This article was unsigned, attributed only to: 'One Who Thinks He Knows'. Its authorship would have astonished Vittoria Cremers, for *this* was the very same piece that had excited Blavatsky, and her companions so much. This is the piece that they had all wrongly imagined was written *by* the Karl of Crawford. But it was by D'Onston, who was paid the glorious sum of £4 for it. Four pounds, for an article which is at once a veiled confession and a tantalizing exercise in misdirection! His authorship was partly revealed in an amusing fragment written by W. T. Stead, on 3 December 1888:

Mr Arthur Diosy is aggrieved. The ingenious contributor who discovered the nationality of the Whitechapel murderer said that no one had hit upon the suggested necromantic motive. Mr Diosy says he mid the police all about it on Oct 14, which of course is news to everybody else. He also darkly hints that the dates of the crimes have some occult relation to

magical astrology. It would be more to the point if Mr Diosy would tell us where the next murder ought to occur according to the dates of magical astrology.

'One who Thinks he Knows' - the contributor in question - is an occultist of some experience. When he was a lad of eighteen he studied necromancy under the late Lord Lytton at Alexandria. It would be odd if the mystical lore of the author of 'Zanoni' were to help unearth Jack the Ripper.

Here Stead is slightly confused, since Lytton's Lodge of Alexandria was based in London, not Egypt, but this is of minor importance. This same article also brought to light details of a series of sexual serial murders even more hideous than those recorded in Austin, Texas. These details came in a letter published in *Pall Mall* on 12 December 1888. The writer had seen the reprint of the article in the *Pall Mall Budget* of 6 December 1888, and wrote:

'JACK THE RIPPER'S' MOTIVE

Sir, - Although the anxiety to solve the Whitechapel mystery is, for the nonce, allayed, if not extinct, it may interest students of human nature to hear of a somewhat similar case in which the murderer, when discovered, was found to be actuated by a less extraordinary motive than that of solving necromantic problems, attributed to the Whitechapel monster by the writer of 'Who is the Whitechapel Demon', published in your issue of the 6th inst. Forty or fifty years ago, my grandfather, a Portuguese judge at Coviltra, convicted a man for the murder of sixteen women by stabbing them in the abdomen. For the space of twelve months the inhabitants of the town had been in a state of wild panic at the periodical repetition of such hideous and objectless crimes, as in no case could pillage or lust be ascribed as cause; the victims, in many cases, being penniless octogenarians. At last the miscreant was caught in flagrante delicto, *and on trying him for wilful murder Judge Joao de Campes received from him the confession that he had done it solely to enjoy the fun of watching the grimaces the poor women made in their agony! I have no details of the criminal's* modus operands *as it occurred long before my time; I had in fact forgotten this episode in my grandfather's judicial career until the accounts of the London ghastly tragedies brought to my mind the conviction that should the East-end murderer ever be brought to justice, which I do not anticipate, it will be ascertained that his motive has been either a morbid taste of the very same kind, or an exaggerated longing for notoriety, coupled with the love of excitement that feeds on perusing the different versions of his deeds, his intentions, and the means he employs to defeat the combined intellects of the detective administrations of London, which last feat, be it said, might make anybody a little proud.*

Yours faithfully, Esther Delaforce, *9 Courthope-villa, Wimbledon*

Esther Delaforce drew some shrewd conclusions in her letter, but it is doubtful if anyone at the time realized the mocking nature of D'Onston's article. Indeed its full significance can only be fully grasped today. Only now are we able to cross-reference his various statements. Only now can we match his conduct with that of the many other serial killers whose patterns have been assessed and profiled.

What, then does he have to say for himself? What lies behind the taunts?

Chapter 28

The Tangled Truth

The *Pall Mall* article shows D'Onston in an arrogant, mocking mood. He sets off to unfold a freshly developed theory and writes as if the Black Magic aspect is something new to him. Yet we now know that he had studied the subject for well over twenty years. Then he rules out English villainy and points the finger at a Frenchman. So what is he is up to?

Behind the smokescreen of words is the simple boast: 'You are deceived by a man devoted to Black Magic; a man who is a linguist; an educated man; a Frenchman'. Had he placed his name to the article, readers would have seen the French connection at once. Had they glimpsed his letter to the City Police they would have known that he was alluding to someone who '… frequented the East End for years…' Someone who may well have '…written (the message) to throw a false scent'. He is in fact pointing the finger at himself, but in a safe way. By placing absurdities in his account he makes it look like the musings of an inept armchair detective. It ceases to look like the work of an insider. And yet his absurdities are grotesque. He states that the writing on the wall was written '…just above the body of the murdered woman…' None of the papers he read at the time made that blunder. Then he adds in the Tabram killing, strikes the Kelly murder out of the reckoning and fools around by introducing the body 'found in the new police-buildings'.

Now these are not his *real* views. We know from Cremers that he gave the true number of murders as five. We know from her that he was adamant that these murders had ended with Kelly. We know further that he insisted that there were no more murders to come. And there speaks *the insider*. All around him people were inflating the figures: seven, nine, twelve, fourteen. But he knew there were five only. We can now recognize that this article was simply the second stage in a planned campaign of misinformation.

The third stage was reached after he left the London Hospital on 7 December 1888. From his hospital bed he had written to Editor Stead and asked for financial assistance to hunt down the Ripper. That was in November. He then made contact with the City police and wrote his notable Whitechapel piece. So he was, on the surface, eager and keen to cash in on the murders. Any good journalist would have been. But on 7 December, at the very time when a new murder could have been expected, D'Onston *left* the East End! Every other journalist stayed put, waiting for the next horror, but not him. On leaving the hospital he moved away from White

chapel and moved to quarters just off St Martin's Lane, north of Trafalgar Square. His new-found indifference to the murder area showed that no further murders were planned - just yet. His actions were exactly those of someone who dealt in certainties.

Once settled into his new rooms, he began to engineer the boldest part of his plan. He decided to add to the confusion and bring matters to a head. This decision may well have been forced on him by an odd story that fellow- journalists were working on at this time. The basic elements of this story involved a letter sent by a patient at a London hospital. The writing was said to resemble that of the original Ripper missives. The sender was a man well acquainted with the East End, with contacts among the rescue and mission workers there. These things, and more, had led to a police interest and a look-out for the man.

Now, this outline description fitted D'Onston. Easily. His contacts among the mission workers began when he edited sermons for the late Rev. Alex McAuslane; and his handwriting did look similar to that on the two original Ripper items. But though he knew those Ripper pieces were hoaxes, he also knew

> " The murderer would induce a woman to go up a back street or room and to excite his passion would 'bugger' her and cut her throat at the same time with his right hand, holding on by the left "

that many took them seriously. So it was now time to disengage himself from all danger. Time to make the first move, and deliberately court suspicion. Time to involve himself in a time-wasting charade so that the police would dismiss him completely. Time to meet the police face to face.

His plan was simple. First find a gullible dupe who would take in every lurid tale told him. Talk to him often and vividly enough and let him feel that the talker knew just too much. Such a dupe would fly to the police and unburden himself quite soon. In seeking out such a dupe D'Onston struck good fortune; he met impressionable George Marsh.

Marsh was an unemployed man with dreams of becoming a private detective, but he was no match for D'Onston's cunning. They drank together almost nightly and D'Onston fed him a strange tale about the murders. He said he knew the killer well, and even named him as a

Dr Davies. Then he described the techniques used in the murders, and revelled in his descriptions.

But D'Onston knew all about suggestibility and he saw to it that Marsh would soon reject the idea of Davies as the killer. His subterfuge was rewarded. Marsh was swayed by the sheer realism of D'Onston's descriptions and drew his own conclusions; he came to believe that he was talking to the killer himself. Only an 'insider' could have such a fee for the murders and radiate such certainties about them. This was no overnight conviction, hut when it came it was all the stronger for the delay.

D'Onston proved to be an astute psychologist and judge of men. Marsh became so excited by the encounters that within three weeks he went to Scotland Yard and fingered *D'Onston* as the Ripper. This fitted D'Onston's plans exactly. Marsh's statement, dictated to Inspector J. Roots on Christmas Eve 1888, read:

*A*bout a month ago at Prince Albert public house, Upper St Martin's Lane, I met a man named Stephenson and casually discussed the murders in Whitechapel with him. From that time to the present I have met him there two or three times a week and we have on each occasion discussed the murders in a confidential manner. He has tried to tell me how I could capture the man if I went his way to work. I simply told him I should go my own way about it and sooner or later I'd have him. I told him I was an amateur detective and that I had been for weeks looking for the culprit. He explained to me how the murders were committed. He said they were committed by a woman-hater after the forthcoming manner:-

The murderer would induce a woman to go up a back street or room and to excite his passion would 'bugger' her and cut her throat at the same time with his right hand, holding on by the left.

He illustrated the action. From his manner I am of the opinion he is the murderer in the first six cases, if not the last one.

Today Stephenson told me that Dr Davies of Houndsditch (I don't know the address although I have been there and could point it out) was the murderer and he wished me to see him. He drew up an agreement to share the reward on the conviction of Dr Davies. I know that agreement is valueless but it secured his handwriting. I made him under the influence of drink thinking that I should get some further statement but in this I failed as he left to see Dr Davies and also to go to Mr Stead of the Pall Mall Gazette with an article for which he expected £2. He wrote the article in the Pall Mall Gazette in relation to the writing on the wall about Jews. He had £4 for that. I have seen letters from Mr Stead in his possession about it; also a letter from Mr Stead refusing to allow him money to find out the Whitechapel Murderer.

Stephenson has shown me a discharge as a patient from the London Hospital. The name Stephenson is obliterated and that of Davies is marked in red ink. I do not know the date.

Stephenson is now at the common lodging house No. 29 Castle St., St Martins Lane, WC, and has been there three weeks. His description is: Age 48, Height 5ft 10in, full face, sallow complexion, moustache heavy - mouse coloured - waxed and turned up, hair brown turning grey, eyes sunken. When looking at a stranger generally has an eyeglass. Dress, grey suit and light brown felt hat - all well worn; military appearance: says he has been in 42 battles: well educated.

The agreement he gave me I will leave with you and will render any assistance the Police may require.

Stephenson is not a drunkard: he is what I call a regular soaker - can drink from 8 o'clock in the morning until closing time but keep a clear head.

The 'agreement' referred to by Marsh is a tongue-in-cheek missive scribbled out on a scrap of paper by D'Onston. It reads ' I hereby agree to pay to Dr R. D'O. Stephenson (also known as 'Sudden Death') one half of any or all the rewards or monies received by me on a/c of the conviction of Dr Davies for wilful murder.'

It should be noted that this was one of the rare occasions when D'Onston used his real family name, and he had a good reason for this, since he knew the document would land on the desk of an old friend of his at the Yard. As for the use of the nickname 'Sudden Death', this was a minor stroke of genius. It has no bearing on the murders. It is nothing but a weird card- gambling term along with others like 'Suicide Squeeze' and 'Cannibal Squeeze' and its use simply confirms that, like his mentor Lord Lytton, he was addicted to the card-tables. But by using it on that agreement he made the whole transaction look childish and foolish; like a game of solemn make-believe between two reeling drinkers.

Two days after Marsh made his move, D'Onston went in person to the Yard and wrote out his own lengthy statement implicating the unfortunate Dr Davies:

I beg to draw your attention to the attitude of Dr Morgan Davies of... Houndsditch, E. with respect to these murders. But my suspicions attach to him principally in connection with the last one - committed indoors.

Three weeks ago, I was a patient in the London Hospital, in a private ward.. .with a Dr Evans, suffering from typhoid, who used to be visited almost nightly by Dr Davies, when the murders were our usual subject of conversation.

Dr Davies always insisted on the fact that the murder was a man of sexual powers almost effete, which could only be bought into action by some strong stimulus - such as sodomy. He was very positive on this point, that the murderer performed on the women from behind - in fact, per ano. At that time he could have had no information, any more than myself, about the fact that the post-mortem examination revealed that semen was found up the woman's rectum, mixed with her faeces.

Many things, which would seem trivial in writing, seemed to me to connect him with the affair — for instance, he is himself a woman- hater. Although a man of powerful frame, &, (according to the lines on his sallow face) of strong sexual passions. He is supposed, however, by his inmates, never to touch a woman. One night, when five medicos were present, quietly discussing the subject, & combating his argument that the murderer did not do these things to obtain specimens of uteri (wombs) but that - in his case - it was the lust of murder developed from sexual lust - a thing not unknown to medicos, he acted (in a way which fairly terrified those five doctors) the whole scene. He took a knife, 'buggered' an imaginary woman, cut her throat from behind; then, when she was apparently laid prostrate, ripped and slashed her in all directions in a perfect frenzy.

Previously to this performance I had said: After a man had done a thing like this, reaction would take place, & he would collapse, & be taken at once to the police, or would attract the attention of the bystanders by his exhausted condition?' Dr - said 'NO! he would recover himself when the fit was over & be as calm as a lamb. I will show you!' Then he began his performance. At the end of it he stopped, buttoned up his coat, put on his hat, and walked down the room with the most perfect calmness. Certainly his face was as pale as death, but that was all.

It was only a few days ago, after I was positively informed by the Editor of the Pall Mall Gazette that the murdered woman last operated on had been sodomized - that I thought - 'How did he know?' His acting was the most vivid I ever saw. Henry Irving was a fool to it. Another point. He argued that the murderer did not want specimens of uteri, but grasped them & slashed them & slashed them off in his madness as being the only hard substance which met his grasp, when his hands were madly plunging into the abdomen of his victim.

I may say that Dr Davies was for some time House Physician at the London Hospital Whitechapel, that lie has lately taken this house in Castle St., Houndsditch; that lie has lived in the locality of the murders for some years; & that he professes his intention of going to Australia shortly should he not quickly make a success in his new house.

Roslyn D'O Stephenson

PS I have mentioned this matter to a pseudo-detective named George Marsh of 24 Pratt St., Camden Town NW, with whom I have made an agreement (enclosed herewith) to share any reward which he may derive from my information.

There is no record of the inquiries prompted by this statement, once again the records are incomplete. But, as we have seen, there is nothing sinister in this.

What we do know is that no action was taken against Dr Davies. After checking the tale the police most likely concluded that the account was simply drawn from fevered memories brought on by hospital medication. That, naturally, is what they were meant to conclude. But we do learn one important thing from this visit. We discover that Marsh had actually been interviewed by a long-time friend of D'Onston's, Inspector Roots.

This is too much to explain away by a mere coincidence. The Inspector's name must have been brought to Marsh's mind during one of the drinking bouts. By leading Marsh to ask for the right man, D'Onston minimized the difficulties for himself. As Roots' own statement shows, he had a sneaking admiration for the Bohemian journalist; he may well have been one of D'Onston's referees at the time of his Orphanage application. Inspector Roots' report is short but of great interest and value:

With reference to the statement of Mr George Marsh of 24th inst., regarding the probable association of Dr Davies and Stephenson with the murders in Whitechapel.

I beg to report that Dr Stephenson came here this evening and wrote the attached statement of his suspicions of Dr Morgan Davies, Casde St., Houndsditch; and also left with me his agreement with Marsh as to the reward. I attach it.

When Marsh came here on 24th I was under the impression that Stephenson was a man I had known 20 years. I now find that impression was correct. He is a travelled man of education and ability, a doctor of medicine upon diplomas of Paris & New York: a major from the Italian Army — he fought under Garibaldi: and a newspaper writer. He says that he wrote the article about Jews in the Pall Mall Gazette, that he occasionally writes for that paper, and that he offered his services to Mr Stead to track the murderer. He showed me a letter from Mr Stead, dated Nov. 30 1888, about this and said that the result was that the proprietor declined to engage upon it. He has lead a Bohemian life, drinks very heavily, and always carries drugs to sober him and stave off delirium tremens.

He was an applicant for the Orphanage Secretaryship at the last election.

> " As we have seen, they were looking for the proverbial madman, not for a quiet-spoken, cultured gentleman "

All these important papers on D'Onston were not unearthed until 1974, when BBC programme-makers were allowed to view many of the then-closed files. But they were just a few sheets among many and were regarded as oddities. Their dates show that D'Onston made his move just in time, for on 30 December 1888, the *Sunday Times* revealed some of the details of the investigation that had alerted and alarmed D'Onston. As summarized by *Pall Mall,* this story ran:

...a gentleman who has for some time been engaged in philanthropic work in the East-end recently received a letter, the handwriting of which had previously attracted the attention of the Post-office authorities on account of its similarity to that of the writer of some of the letters signed 'Jack the Ripper'. The police made inquiries, and ascertained that the writer was known to his correspondent as a person intimately acquainted with East-end life, and that he was then a patient in a metropolitan hospital. It is stated that on an inquiry at the hospital it was discovered that the person sought had left without the consent or knowledge of the hospital authorities, but that he has been subsequently seen, and is now under observation. The police are of the opinion that the last five murders were a series, and that the first two were independently perpetrated.

Was the suspect mentioned in that article D'Onston himself? Or were the resemblances purely coincidental? There is no sure answer to those questions, but we do know that D'Onston was taken in for questioning on two occasions. Yet he was more than a match for the police. As we have seen, they were looking for the proverbial madman, not for a quiet-spoken, cultured gentleman, well accustomed to using words to conceal and reveal. He may well have seemed an oddity to them, but never for a moment did he look like a gory knife-man. And yet, had they but read his later articles in *Pall Mall* they would have seen something of his darker side. They would have read the words of someone who openly admitted killing a woman.

Chapter 29

From the Pen
of the Ripper

The black year of 1888 ended with some false alarms but no dramatic arrests. For a while D'Onston lay low and provoked no further mischief. Then, in January 1889, he was commissioned to write an article for Pall Mall, dealing with the real-life background of Rider Haggard's book She. It appeared on 3 January, and in it, he dealt with the magical cults of the West Coast of Africa. In particular he wrote: '...whatever you have read of magical powers — especially those of necromancy - are absolutely possible; absolutely true; absolutely accomplished!'

These words from a complete believer attracted so much interest and correspondence that Stead commissioned a second article, which he ran front page on 15 February 1889. In this new piece D'Onston first amplifies his dramatic views on devil worship:

...that is, the use of rites, ceremonies, adjurations, and hymns to the powerful and personal spirit of evil, whose favour is obtained by means of orgies which for horror, blasphemy and obscenity cannot have ever been exceeded - if indeed they have ever been equalled, in the history of the world. These things are too utterly horrible even to be hinted at. It is the fashion at present to deny the existence of Satan, Shaitan, Ahrimanes (or whatever you please to call the incarnation of all evil. But all occults, of whatever school, know that everything in Nature has its counter-

> ❝Her death then and her 'absolute annihilation' was a necessary evil❞

part, that you cannot have light without shadow, heat without cold, good without evil, nor yet a personal Deity without an equally personal evil principle.

Later in this article he describes the amazing powers of a malevolent woman witch-doctor in the Cameroons, who imprisoned him. Then he claims that he eliminated her; that he was the means '... not only of her death, but of her absolute annihilation'.

How he killed the woman is not clear. Yet the manner of her death is of small account. What is of importance is his cold-blooded recording of the deed, and the fact that revelled in it. Few normal men would have boasted of such a deed *in print,* but this was *a* man without guilt or remorse. This confession **to** killing a woman was made in such a casual fashion that its impact was smothered. But this was his style. This is what he wanted. Think back to his revelations to Cremers. Remember how he spoke of his brutalities in America, and his butchery in Italy. Everything, then, was delivered in a superior throw-away manner, hiding all signs of any gloating pleasure.

This is exactly how he revealed the killing in his article. There he dismissed his guilt by arguing that the witch-doctor was intent on killing him. Her death then and her 'absolute annihilation' was a necessary evil. So, with a single masterstroke he justified his actions, and satisfied his burning drive to confess and savour his crimes. All this without one word of regret; a man without a soul.

Since no reader protested against his presentation, it seems that his tactic worked. But this confession further illuminates his character. It is a public affirmation that he *was* prepared to kill a woman any time it suited his interests, and without pangs of conscience.

Later, in November 1890, another of his articles on 'African Magic' appeared in *Lucifer,* a magazine meant for a quite restricted readership. This encouraged D'Onston to open up in a bolder way for in his piece he spells out the differences between White and Black Magic, his words apply not just to Africa, but universally; in particular they embrace the Whitechapel killings, for he states:

> *...the necromancer must outrage and degrade human nature in every way conceivable. The very least of the crimes necessary for him (or her) to commit to attain the power sought is actual murder, by which the human victim essential to the sacrifice is provided...Yet, though the price is awful, horrible, unutterable, the power is real. There is no possibility of mistake about that.*

Murder to gain power; this is the message straight from the pen of a man steeped in the traditions of Black Magic. But these are the ideas he had nursed for years; the very ideas that had fired the sexual lusts behind his killings. For ultimately, all lust-murder is an exercise of supreme merciless power. But whatever dynamic powers he sought to draw on 1888, they had failed him totally in the year following the murders. 1889 began for him on a hateful note. On 5 January his father died and left him nothing at all; the late for his father had been returned with full bitterness.

Then, on Monday 13 May, D'Onston was taken into the London Hospital seriously ill, suffering from an acute bout: of 'chloralism'; not surprising for a man who had pushed himself to the limits. Chloralism is a paralysed state of the system brought on by the immoderate or prolonged use of chloral hydrate. This drug is little used today in medicine, though it is still slyly introduced into drinks in the underworld; in fact, it is the basis of 'knockout drops' or 'Mickey Finns'. Used in large and repeated doses it causes delirium, hallucinations, and a state of coma which can lead to cardiac failure.

At the time of his collapse D'Onston was back in the East End. He had moved into the headquarters of the London Cottage Mission in Burdett Road. What special role he played there is unknown. What we do know is that his need for choral hydrate shows that sleep had deserted him. Now the black pit of despondency had opened up. All the hideous killings had taken their toll. Nothing had been gained but wild excitements and tortured memories. And there he was, a bleak nonentity, with his funds draining away and all his dreams of grandeur vanishing. It was then he reached his lowest point ever. Weak and demoralized, he was now incapable of even imagining a new autumn of terror.

It was a grim irony, that the Lon-

Then the two met as equals, and soon blended as lovers.

It was a fateful encounter for Collins. Early hero-worship and elation died fast. Euphoria was quickly overshadowed by remorseless despair as her 'great magician revealed himself as rotten to the core. Stark fear then gripped her. A sadistic killer had ensnared her and enforced her silence. A blind hunger for love had bedded her down with a ghoul.

At the end of the affair and the break-up of the cosmetic business, D'Onston stayed on for a while in Upper Baker Street. He was no longer a kept man and had to fall back on his own resources. It was at this time he began using his full name and his New York medical diploma; whether this implies some type of consultancy is uncertain. His shadowy lifestyle still veils our understanding. But a curious and notable co-incidence occurred at this time.

Going south from his Baker Street rooms D'Onston would have reached the doorstep of 14 York Place within minutes. This was the home of the flamboyant Dr Forbes Winslow, the many *totally* convinced that he knew who the Ripper was. It is bizarre to realize that these two men may well have met each other; and

don Hospital, once the nerve-centre of his triumphs and ruthless plans, now became a cold, clinical refuge for his exhausted mind and body. One event only was to brighten up his seventy- four dreary days spent there; it was a totally unexpected and glowing letter written by Mabel Collins. She was so excited by his African reminiscences that she now ached to meet the author. A meeting was arranged the moment D'Onston was fit.

may even have talked about the murders. I know the Ripper would have enjoyed egging the 'Ripper expert' on to new heights of verbal folly; (or D'Onston would have recognized the doctor at once). Indeed every London journalist knew the vocal and dogmatic doctor. His bombastic words were a treasure for them. So the chance to taunt the pompous poseur would have proved irresistible.

But how long did D'Onston stay in Baker Street? No answer is yet possible. The missing five years baffle us. There is not the slightest trace of the man until 1896. In that year we learn for the first time that Cremers and Collins were not alone in thinking of him as the Ripper. In his quarterly magazine *Borderland,* W. T. Stead introduced some articles by D'Onston with these telling words:

> *He has been known to me for many years. He is one of the most remarkable persons I ever met. For more than a year I was under the impression that he was the veritable Jack the Ripper; an impression which I believe was shared by the police, who at least once had him under arrest; although, as he completely satisfied them, they liberated him without bringing him into court.*

Note those words well. They prove that D'Onston had lowered his guard with Stead and said a little too much. Stead, in turn, began to probe. He must then have uncovered things that showed D'Onston quite capable of murder. And not just ordinary murder, but the grotesque knife-killings that were the hallmark of the Ripper. This conviction stayed with Stead for over a year and made such a deep impression, that eight years later he felt impelled to record it.

What caused Stead to abandon his view? Since no one ever asked him, we have to guess at the reason and it probably stems from the idea that the Ripper went on killing *after* 1888. This belief was held by many newspapers and even Police Commissioner Monro was uncertain.

At first, Monro viewed the McKenzie murder, of July 1889, as 'identical with the notorious Jack the Ripper of last year'. Two months later came the finding of the body under the railway arch, and again Monro speculated that it might be another Ripper victim. Given this confusion, it is likely that D'Onston had an unbreakable alibi for the time of one of the pseudo-Ripper events, and that was enough for Stead to back down.

But is there nothing in D'Onston's ac-

> **" Two months later came the finding of the body under the railway arch, and again Monro speculated that it might be another Ripper victim "**

tions and claims that give us legitimate cause for doubt? To answer that we need to look at some of the problems that appear to be raised by his statement made on Boxing Day 1888 at Scotland Yard. In that statement we find two unexpected claims.

These appear where D'Onston comments on the Kelly murder. He first writes that a post-mortem examination had '...revealed that semen was found up the woman's rectum...' That seems a clear enough statement by any standards. One woman, Kelly, had been shown to have been sodomized. At the end of this document, he reinforces this initial claim by elaborating further, and giving his source: 'It was only a few days ago...!' was positively informed by the Editor of the *Pall Mall Gazette* that the murdered woman *last* operated on had been sodomized...' Again, another clear reference to Kelly, the last to die, and a clear reference to W. T. Stead.

It is hard to see how these two ex-

tremely clear statements could ever be misunderstood, yet they have been. Faulty research by the three authors of *The Jack the Ripper A to Z* has lead them into error. In their book they offer *misreadings* of the original, unambiguous text. They alter D'Onston's meaning and make him seem to refer to a number of victims, instead of just one. Then having done that, they are able to draw false conclusions, leading to the assumption that D'Onston is quite unreliable.

Consider their page 276. It says this of D'Onston: '...he learned (erroneously) from W. T. Stead that the Ripper habitually sodomized his victims'. This misrepresents the basic texts. They appear in full, here, in my book. Anyone can immediately check and see what Stead actually said; that he spoke only of one victim.

The same basic error is repeated in substance on their page 274, which says: 'Stead... accepted articles on the case from Robert D'Onston Stephenson, according to whom he also supplied the

> " In playing his cruel game of words with Cremers, D'Onston was quite emphatic about the sexual aspects of the murders "

information that the victims had been sodomized.'

This misrepresentation is further compounded by a passage on page 64: '...he (D'Onston) learned from W. T. Stead that medical reports showed that the victims had been sodomized (they didn't)...'

If the D'Onston statement is now re-read with due care, it will be seen at once that his claim about Stead is tied to ONE case, and one case only, namely '.. .the last one - committed indoors.. .the murdered woman last operated on...' In other words he is talking about Kelly and Kelly alone. Note that.

Note further, that at no point does D'Onston make mention of any 'medical reports', in truth he does not even speak of a single report; he does no more than state that Stead had informed him that Kelly had been sodomized, and that this was a discovery made in the course of the post-mortem examination.

Now a post-mortem examination can lead to a written report or reports, but it can also involve *discussion* of facts never committed to writing. And it can result in leaks to trusted or valued outsiders. Such leaks can involve information not generally known. Stead had many contacts who gave him this type of information with regularity. This is well known.

Having established that, reconsider Bond's written report on Mary Jane Kelly. No mention of sodomy, certainly, but equally no mention of vaginal intercourse, and no mention of a search for any 'signs of connection'. There is not even a mention of seminal fluids anywhere. But in all logic, sexual activity of one kind or another would have taken place. So the very absence of all mention of sexual traces means that Bond chose not to put his findings in writing. He had the latitude to do this. There were no rigid rules governing the writing of such reports — they could be curt, or highly elaborate and still be acceptable. The contrast between Browns detailed report on Eddowes, and Bond's terse report on Kelly illustrates this perfectly.

Let this be emphasized: Bond's report neither confirms nor negates the information said to have been known to Stead. On this score his report is neutral. On the other hand, though, Bond's very silence makes it possible, indeed highly probable, that he would have extra knowledge to share with confidants.

I accept D'Onston's claim relating to Stead for the very good reason that Stead was the last person that D'Onston could afford to offend. He could not invoke Stead's name in connection with *any* bogus statements, since Stead was his sole source of income and prestige at the time. Once Stead was drawn in, D'Onston had no control over subsequent developments. So his confidence in naming Stead has to rest on firm ground; there would be no comeback. And in fact there wasn't. Far from it. Following the statement and enquiries by the Yard came two good commissions from Stead - a vote of confidence if anything ever was.

As for D'Onston's claim that the victims were 'performed on from behind - in fact, *per and* - in police terms, this is a perfectly acceptable *modus operandi* with nothing in the records to refute it. We need to remember that the sexual rituals will vary in degrees, even if they are staged along similar patterns with predetermined sequences. An act of penetration alone, without orgasm, can count as the symbolic exercise of power. Withdrawal; delayed gratification; onanism proper; all these things can be present at one time and absent at another. That is why I regard Dr Brown's report on Eddowes as equally neutral on the issue of sodomy.

Unlike Bond, Dr Brown did write about his *sexual* findings and stated that he found no traces of recent connection or secretion of any kind on the thighs. Yet, even if he had made such a probe, he would still be in the dark if no semen had been ejected. So 'neutral' is the only sound and just verdict possible.

Having disposed of those meritless objections, what else do we need to clarify? One of the obvious puzzles seems to be the clash between his article with its description of the killings as purely ritual murders, pre-planned to profane the cross; and his later contention when speaking to Marsh, Inspector Roots, and Cremers, that the prime motive was sexual. But these two explanations in fact, harmonize with each other, as we shall see.

D'Onston knew full well that the driving force behind his crude rites and beliefs was a warped sexual impulse. You have only to study the numerous works on magic to see that all sexual yearnings and fears are drawn on repeatedly. Indeed, in the hands of Alaister Crowley magical rites became synonymous with prolonged sexual activities of all types, from sodomy to bestiality. If we reconsider D'Onston's explanation of 1 December we see that it stresses the ritualistic nature of the murders, with the murder-sites marking a cross. Yet in his Scotland Yard statement of 28 December, when he involved 'Dr Davies', the sexual element alone is stressed. At first sight this may seem contradictory, but in fact we are being shown two halves of the same story. This is confirmed beyond doubt by D'Onston's explanation to Cremers, when he seized her from behind and terrified her. He first stated that the doctor's drives were sexual, then he went on to include the ritualistic element, saying:

> He [the doctor] told me that he always selected the place where he intended to murder the women... It was for a very special reason, Vittoria, which you would not understand. He took the Whitechapel Road as a sort of base for his operations, and made several journeys before deciding on the spots best suited to fit in with his scheme of things. Then, having got his victims to these particular places, he manoeuvred to get behind them.

In playing his cruel game of words with Cremers, D'Onston was quite emphatic about the sexual aspects of the murders; so much so that Cremers guessed D'Onston was talking about himself. But even so, he was deliberately evasive about the rituals involved in them.

Unlike Cremers, we have read all of D'Onston's writings, so with hindsight we know that the 'very special reason' mentioned by D'Onston is identical with the ritualistic profaning of the cross detailed in his December piece. His four prime victims were chosen to mark the points of a giant cross thrown across Whitechapel. Let no one balk at the idea of an imaginary cross; millions of Christians create them every day.

Chapter 30

This Man Dodged the Noose

We are now in a position to bring together all that we know about D'Onston and show that his actions and words condemn him utterly. This man is no casual observer at the fringes of the mystery. This man is at the very heart of the mystery.

That he was callous, cold blooded, unmoved by human suffering has been proved beyond doubt. Not a single line written by him speaks of love for humanity. Evil and hate and the macabre were always present in his works, for that was the man.

We know for certain that he slaughtered as a soldier while still impressionable. His licence to slash through flesh and bone, to disembowel, to behead with a sabre stroke, gave him a taste for killing that festered within him. His medical butchery provided practical lessons in anatomy, made him indifferent towards suffering and developed his fast, crude knife work.

His complex, bitter-sweet involvement with a prostitute left him with a raw hatred of all other prostitutes; while his fanatical obsession with Black Magic interlocked with his sexual passions and created perverted drives. So perverted that when they peaked, they led to his carefully planned serial sexual murders. Such careful, even meticulous, planning is one of the essential features of most sexual serial murderers. But what of the other essential features?

Comparing D'Onston with modern serial killers is both revealing and chilling.

Here was a fastidious man bathing every day, brushing his clothes to the point of wear; and yet he preserved those huge black ties in a stained and encrusted condition. These two attitudes don't make sense. They become understandable *only* when we realize that the keeping of fetishist mementos of killings is one of the *hallmarks* of sexual serial killers. And remember that he spoke of the ties ages before Cremers found that they still existed. Joel Norris has drawn attention to both aspects of such compulsive behaviour, saying:

Serial killers and potential serial killers have deeply compulsive personalities, and the compulsivity is manifested in more than one or two ways at a time. Several of the killers researched...had compulsivity concerning their physical appearance. Bobby Joe Long took several showers a day, sometimes as many as six, during most of his adult life even before the motorcycle accident... Carlton Gray was also a compulsive showerer. Leonard Lake also had a compulsivity about being neat and clean around the home, according to his ex-wife Cricket Balazs, who reported that he two often argued about her cleanliness. As part of his murder rite, he forced his victims to take showers prior to their rape and eventual murder.

Many serial killers are also compulsive record-keepers. They maintain scrapbooks and organized memorabilia concerning the killings as well as preserving parts of their victims' bodies or clothing. This pattern is so common among the killers that some homicide detectives feel that the discovery of souvenirs is a high-priority piece of evidence during the instigation. Among the items of memorabilia catalogued by the serial killers in our study were scrapbooks with press clippings of the murders, press clippings of other or similar serial killings, books on psychology and deviant behaviour, books on people who suffered from multiple personalities and manifested violent criminal behaviour, biographies of Hitler and other mass murderers, personal items or body parts of the victims. These are especially indicative of the serial murderer syndrome because the taking of a victim's body part is associate with the ritualistic fantasy and it becomes a totem. Among the items catalogued were teeth, fingers, toes, nipples, breasts and penises. Clothing and underwear were also collected as were snippets of hair, barrettes, and articles of decoration that the victims wore.

In some cases, killers have preserved

out of the skins of his victims and wove bracelets out of their hair.

Did D'Onston preset any of the body parts he took away with him? This would have been quite in keeping with his personality. Those preserved ties, though, were tangible enough and significant enough. They count as the 'high priority' type of evidence that Joel Norris draws attention to.

D'Onston's actions in courting the attention of the police are also mirrored in many modern cases. Edmund Kemper, for one, hung out at a bar near his local Court House and made friends with the policeman using it. By talking to the officers about the unsolved murders (*his* murders), be came to be looked on as a friendly nuisance. 'It was deliberate,' said Kemper. Friendly nuisances are dismissed.' How right he was!

FBI profiler Robert Ressler has summed up this type of post-crime behaviour as something, '...*which in some cases can be quite important, as some offenders attempt to inject themselves into the investigation of the murder, or otherwise keep in touch with the crime in order to continue the fantasy that started it*'.

whole sections of their victim's bodies, such as legs, trunks and torsos. Edmund Kemper, for example, murdered his mother and kept her head... Ed Gein kept his mother's cadaver, which he amateurishly embalmed on the property for many years... He also made lampshades

" But there was a hidden side. Behind that quiet facade lurked the quickness of eye and foot of an old swordsman, a fighter with an iron-willed command of his emotions "

This brings strongly to mind D'Onston's appeal to Stead asking for funds to 'hunt the Ripper'; his letter of 'help' to the City Police sent from his hospital ward; and his 'Dr Davies' statement to Inspector Roots of the Yard, a police officer he'd known for almost twenty years. This is exactly the type of behaviour logged by the FBI.

Even occult trappings are linked with some of the modern serial killers profiled by the FBI. Few of these modern killers show the same intense involvement that we find in D'Onston, but the raw basics are there.

Richard Ramirez, feared as the 'The Night Stalker', and murderer of thirteen people, left a satanic pentagram sketch at the scene of several of his crimes. The still-unknown killer who used the name 'Zodiac', signed some of his taunting letters with a circle overlaid with a cross, an astrological symbol, tied in with his killings.

But D'Onston was a creature of a different time and culture, so we should not look for exact correspondences and we should remember that profiling remains an art and not a science. Even so, everything learned from the FBI studies, points to this man, and this man only. Indeed, everything we have considered so far unites D'Onston's name with these murders; nothing diverges. And everything we know about him fits in perfectly with my master profile. A profile drawn up long before D'Onston was ever considered seriously.

When we look back at his youth in Hull we see the beginning of a pattern. His involvement with the sordid world of the dockside prostitutes showed him their weaknesses. In later years, this gave him an edge. He could lull the Whitechapel drabs into a false sense of security with a few chosen words.

Apart from that, there was nothing in his bearing or manner to raise the slightest sense of alarm. On the contrary, we know for certain that he was a quiet-moving, quiet-spoken man, of unassuming appearance.

But there was a hidden side. Behind that quiet facade lurked 'the quickness of eye and foot of an old swordsman', a fighter with an iron-willed command of his emotions, and a man with a military sense of order.

Of his capacity to scheme and organize, there are no doubts. He 'possessed a cool, logical brain and iron nerve'. With the geography of Whitechapel etched into his memory, he planned all his moves with military precision.

Few people have ever pictured the Ripper in this way. The vacant or slobbering madman has dominated thoughts for far too long. Yet, over twenty-eight years ago, long before the Scotland Yard material on D'Onston came to light, the American author, Tom Cullen gave this surprisingly accurate picture of the Ripper:

...he undoubtedly was quiet-spoken, with nothing in his looks or manner to attract attention, let alone to raise alarm... Here was someone who knew how to approach prostitutes without arousing their suspicion, who could talk their language, catch them off guard. And it should be remembered that the whores who worked in Whitechapel were in a state bordering on hysteria... He had studied the terrain as a general might study a situation map.

Without knowing it, Cullen has described D'Onston incisively.

Until recently, the full facts of D'Onston's life remained elusive. Now the essential records have given up their secrets, the case against D'Onston is so compelling that we can say with certainty that he was the killer.

> **" He undoubtedly was quiet-spoken, with nothing in his looks or manner to attract attention, let alone to raise alarm "**

If we take the many-stranded case against him step-by-step, then concentrate on the periods just before and after the murders, we can see that his every move, his every statement written or spoken brands him as *the insider.*

When we summarize his life we can see that the seeds of destruction were sown at an early stage:

In his teens, the magical teachings provided by Lord Lytton gave him warped dreams of glory.

The brutal conflict in Italy gave his cruel streak a free rein.

Back home, the end of his sole love affair killed all tenderness within him.

The death of prostitute Ada-Louise fuelled his hatred of the harlotry that had doomed his lover's life.

His family cut him off from their money and influence. In revenge he married his mother's maid and confirmed himself as an outcast.

His megalomania grew. His obsession with magic convinced him that he could elevate his status and astonish the world.

Yet greatness eluded him. His thoughts became more compulsive and corrosive. Even the extremes of Black Magic became inviting. Only his wife stood in the way, but not for long.

In 1887, his wife 'vanished' without trace. Had he murdered her? He implied that he had. So was it *her* death that finally triggered off the spate of other deaths in Whitechapel?

With his wife eliminated, he posed as single, and feigning illness returned to Whitechapel. There in his ideal hospital retreat, he lay within easy reach of each planned murder-site. And then the murders began.

D'Onston needed no nickname, he killed anonymously. While the world was convinced and horrified by the 'Jack the Ripper' letter and postcard, he completely ignored them. They were not from his pen. They were nothing but empty hoaxes.

When he did write, it was simply to inject himself into the inquiry. This tactic began even before the last murder was staged. Letters to Stead and the City Police began the charade. Then followed his infamous Calvary Cross article of December.

Of all the journalists he was the only one to *insist* that the notorious writing on the wall had used the word 'Juwes' and had used an eccentric grammar. 'This points to a Frenchman', D'Onston teased.

But D'Onston always knew more than the other involved journalists. He even turned his back on Whitechapel, and left at the very time when all the other newsmen remained, certain that the killer would strike again. But he knew better and his colleagues waited in vain.

He was adamant that the killings were the *sexually* inspired deeds of a sophisticated man, never the work of a madman. At that time, only the Ripper himself could affirm that with such certainty.

He said that there would be no more Ripper murders; and there were none. Only the killer himself could speak with such authority.

With the same authority he told Cremers that the murders were five in number, and five only. In 1890 no one except the killer knew that; and for many years to come, right up until the 1960s, few people would even guess that the number was so low.

After confessing his guilt to Mabel Collins, he silenced her successfully with potent Satanic threats. He tongue-tied the only person able to denounce him.

At Scotland Yard he toyed with the police. Having drawn attention to himself, he deflected suspicion by issuing statements that looked wildly extravagant. He was easy to dismiss.

LEFT Lord Lytton

> "A weird uncanny creature who would come into the office and sit in silence without uttering a word until I could see him.... nerveless and with a calm that nothing would disturb, I should imagine."

But in the long run, he escaped the police simply because they were blind to the true nature of his killer-impulses. Yet others did see through to the terrifying evil within him. We have their testimony.

Though D'Onston dodged the noose he failed to silence the voice of condemnation within himself. Remember his words '....*you cannot have...a personal Deity without an equally personal evil principle*'? Now these words came home to him in a poignant way. He had embraced the evil principle, but like so many other transgressors he grew to want a form of absolution. Like Saul on the road to Damascus he experienced the anguish and relief of religious conversion.

He was not the first killer to be moved in this way. Prison records are full of accounts of such 'brands plucked from the burning'. In his case he would have been well aware of the tremendous promises made by the clerics who surrounded him. Promises that offered redemption even to the lowest of all. Did he heed these famous words of Dr Spurgeon?

There is no sort of a man, there is no abortion of mankind, no demon in human shape, that Christ's blood cannot wash. Hell may have sought to make a paragon of iniquity, it may have striven to put sin and sin together, till it has made a monster abhorred even of mankind; but the blood of Christ can transform that monster... No case can exceed its virtue, be it ever so black or vile.

Once converted, this man, whose writings had never echoed a single Christian sentiment, now devoted himself to the strangest of all tasks.

For years he toiled away at a slim volume of atonement. It was a scholarly study of the Holy Gospels as they existed in the second century. Increasingly troubled by ill-health, he pored over hundreds of ancient and modern texts in many tongues and in 1904 finally completed his only book: *The Patristic Gospels*. It was published by Grant Richards, and in its foreword D'Onston wrote this of his years of work: '...most of this time has been one long fight against pain and paralysis; and nothing but the undeniable aid of the Holy Spirit could have enabled them to have been completed single-handed, and without assistance whatever from anyone.'

His book was hardly a bestseller, but it was never meant to be more than a convert's penance, and soon after it appeared, D'Onston became a man of mystery once more. He simply *vanished* without trace. Despite repeat searches no death certificate can be found within the British Isles or anywhere else. No memoirs or letters tell us how he survived, how long he lived, or how he met his end.

The last person known to have had contact with him was his publisher, Grant Richards, who remembered him well as:

A weird uncanny creature who would come into the office and sit in silence without uttering a word until I could see him. When he was shown in he would scarcely open his mouth beyond asking for an advance of payment on his book. I felt sure D'Onston was not his real name. He was a quiet, calculating sort of fellow, nerveless and with a calm that nothing would disturb, I should imagine.

And that was almost everything that his publisher had to say, except for one passing thought: at one time D'Onston had spoken of moving to Paris. Paris; the place of his student days; the venue of his fateful meeting with Lord Lytton's son. The city that had a special allure unmatched in all Europe.

Does Paris, then, hold the secret of D'Onston's last days? Did he find a retreat there, teaching English from the comfort of an armchair? To these questions there are still no answers, so my original conclusion still stands: 'We may not know how and when D'Onston died, but this much is certain: the Ripper died the moment D'Onston was born again.'

Design & Artwork: ALEX YOUNG

Published by: DEMAND MEDIA LIMITED

Publisher: JASON FENWICK

Written by: MELVYN HARRIS